科技英语入门
（第二版）

主　编：凌惜勤　黄晓玲
副主编：莫金旺　袁颂岳　陈　英
　　　　李　丹　史双喜

苏州大学出版社
Soochow University Press

图书在版编目(CIP)数据

科技英语入门 / 凌惜勤,黄晓玲主编. —2 版. —苏州:苏州大学出版社,2014.8(2017.1 重印)
ISBN 978-7-5672-1054-7

Ⅰ.①科… Ⅱ.①凌… ②黄… Ⅲ.①科学技术－英语 Ⅳ.①H31

中国版本图书馆 CIP 数据核字(2014)第 194040 号

书　　名	科技英语入门(第二版)
主　　编	凌惜勤　黄晓玲
责任编辑	杨　华
装帧设计	刘　俊
出版发行	苏州大学出版社(Soochow University Press)
出 版 人	张建初
社　　址	苏州市十梓街 1 号　邮编:215006
印　　刷	宜兴市盛世文化印刷有限公司
网　　址	www.sudapress.com
E-mail	yanghua@suda.edu.cn
邮购热线	0512-67480030
销售热线	0512-65225020
开　　本	787 mm×960 mm　1/16　印张:12.75　字数:223 千
版　　次	2014 年 8 月第 1 版
印　　次	2017 年 1 月第 2 次印刷
书　　号	ISBN 978-7-5672-1054-7
定　　价	28.00 元

凡购本社图书发现印装错误,请与本社联系调换。服务热线:0512-65225020

第二版编写说明

1. 教材说明

本教材共分 10 个单元，内容包含数学和物理学、计算机科学、计算机网络、模拟电子技术、数字逻辑电路、通信工具、通信调制、机械、汽车、材料学科等理工科题材。

第一单元为数学和物理学。主要介绍了一些基本的、常见的数学和物理学方面的英语词汇，同时介绍了数学和物理学的兴起、发展及其分支。

第二单元介绍了计算机软件知识。作为工科学生，对计算机软件方面的基本英语词语有所掌握还是必须的。同时本单元还详细介绍了如何用计算机来处理实际问题，也就是软件的设计过程。第三单元介绍了计算机网络知识。随着信息时代的发展，信息交流量也与日俱增，因此我们选择介绍了部分网络知识。

第四单元和第五单元则是对电子电路知识的介绍，包括了模拟电路知识和数字电路知识。这两个单元中，从基本的电子元器件入手，直到整体电路的介绍，由浅入深，对整个电子电路方面进行了系统的介绍。

第六单元和第七单元是对通信基本知识的介绍。第六单元介绍了目前通信领域使用非常广泛的软件 MATLAB，第七单元则详细阐述了通信调制。这两个单元中有大量的、基本的通信专业英文术语，同时也结合生产实际对滤波器的设计进行了详细的介绍。

第八单元、第九单元及第十单元分别介绍了机械、汽车和材料学科的一些基本概念，以及这些领域的研究范畴。

2. 教材特色

目前市场上流传着多种版本的科技英语教材。如何使我们所编写的科技英语教材与市场上已有的教材相较更有特色,这是编写过程中重点考虑的问题。

本教材最大的特色就是在口语方面进行了较多尝试,每章都配备了针对本单元主题和文章内容的口语题目,供教师在上课时有选择性地进行师生、生生等口语交流练习。

本教材取材广泛,覆盖了理工科绝大部分基础知识。

本教材各单元选排合理、严谨、科学。每一单元包括 4 篇课文,其中,Passage A 和 Passage B 是精读课文,之后为 Notes,Key words and phrases,Exercises 和 Extended reading。Extended reading 中包含两篇泛读课文,即 Passage C 和 Passage D,要求学生在课后能独立阅读。在这两篇课文后,也给出了部分生词的注解。

本教材注重实用性、先进性。例如,在每单元后都编写了 Application writing,以引导学生用英语完成对一些应用问题的写作;通信单元介绍的 MATLAB 所设计的滤波器的方法在通信领域就是比较领先的。

本教材强调学生思考为主,教师讲解为辅。在每单元前,都有本单元的目标,让学生根据这些目标带着问题去预习和思考,这样有利于进一步开发学生独立学习的能力。

大量练习题目也是本教材的一个特色。英语的学习是比较枯燥的,学生所做的练习往往都是阅读理解、词汇填空。我们一改平常的做法,引入了大量的新题型,其中判断改错就是一种新题型,它要求的并不是修改语法方面的错误,而是修改有关专业知识的错误,这样让学生涉猎一些科技方面的知识,从而激发学生专业英语学习的兴趣。

此次尝试科技英语教材的编写是我们对平时教学的一次深入思考,其中不当之处敬请同行及读者多加指正!

编 者

2014 年 6 月

Contents 目录

Unit One	Mathematics and Physics	(1)
Unit Two	Computer Science	(19)
Unit Three	Computer Networks	(40)
Unit Four	Analog Electronics	(62)
Unit Five	Digital Logic Circuits	(79)
Unit Six	An Important Communication Tool—MATLAB	(102)
Unit Seven	Communication Modulation	(116)
Unit Eight	Mechanics	(131)
Unit Nine	Automobile	(146)
Unit Ten	Materials and Forming Technology	(171)

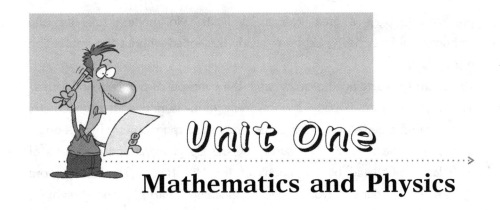

Unit One
Mathematics and Physics

Goals

After studying the unit, you should be able to
- describe the branches of mathematics.
- explain the differences between the axiom and definition of mathematics.
- describe the branches of physics.
- describe the first, second and third laws of motion.
- explain the differences between dynamics and statics.

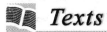 Texts

■ Passage A

Mathematics

Mathematics comes from man's social practice, for example, industrial and agricultural production, commercial activities, **military** operations and scientific and technological researches. And in turn, mathematics serves the practice and plays a great role in all fields. No modern scientific and technological branches could be regularly developed without the application of mathematics.

From the early need of man came the concepts of numbers and forms. Then, **geometry** developed out of problems of measuring land, **trigonometry** came from problems of surveying. Geometry and trigonometry had its origin long ago in the measure and survey by the Babylonians and Egyptians of their lands inundated by the floods of the Nile River. The Greek word "geometry" is derived from "geo", meaning "earth", and "metry", meaning "measure". As early as 2000 BC, we find the land surveyors of these people re-establishing vanishing landmarks and boundaries by utilizing the truths of geometry.[1] Geometry and trigonometry are a science that deals with forms made by lines. A study of geometry and trigonometry is an essential part of the training of the successful engineer, scientist, architect, and draftsman.[2] The carpenter, machinist, stonecutter, artist, and designer all apply the facts of geometry and trigonometry in their trades. Later, to deal with some more complex practical problems, man established and then solved equation with unknown numbers, thus **algebra** occurred. Before the 17th century, man confined himself to the elementary mathematics, i. e. geometry, trigonometry and algebra, in which only the **constants** were considered.

The rapid development of industry in the 17th century promoted the progress of economics and technology and required dealing with **variable quantities**. The leap from constants to variable quantities brought about two new branches of mathematics—analytic geometry and **calculus**, which belong to the higher mathematics. Now there are many branches in higher mathematics, among which are mathematical analysis, higher algebra, **differential** equations, function theory and so on. The study of differential equations is one part of mathematics that, perhaps more than any other, has been directly inspired by mechanics, astronomy, and mathematical physics. Its history began in the 17th century when Newton, Leibniz and

Bernoulli solved some simple differential equations arising from problems in geometry and mechanics.[3] These early discoveries, beginning about in 1690, gradually led to the development of a lot of "special tricks" for solving certain special kinds of differential equations. Although these special tricks are applicable in relatively few cases, they do enable us to solve many differential equations that arise in mechanics and geometry, so their study is of practical importance.

Mathematicians study conceptions and propositions. Axioms, postulates, definitions and theorems are all propositions. Notations are a special and powerful tool of mathematics and are used to express conceptions and propositions very often. Formulas, figures and charts are full of different symbols. Some of the best known symbols of mathematics are the Arabic numerals 1, 2, 3, 4, ... , and the signs of addition " + ", subtraction " − ", less " < ", sigma " Σ ", inequality " $\neq$ ", and so on.

The conclusions in mathematics are obtained mainly by logical deductions and computation. For a long period of the history of mathematics, the centric place of mathematical methods was occupied by the logical deductions.[4] Now, since electronic computers are developed promptly and used widely, the role of computation becomes more and more important. In our times, computation is not only used to deal with a lot of information and data, but also to carry out some work that merely could be done earlier by logical deductions, for example, the proof of most of geometrical theorems.[5]

■ Passage B

Physics

Physics is the study of the properties of matter and energy. Physicists try to understand the universe by searching for the basic laws of nature. They do this by performing experiments. Then they propose a law that explains the results of these experiments. The proposed law can be used to predict other effects. These effects must also be tested by experiment. If they fit the proposed law, then the law becomes established. Most laws have been shown to be at least slightly inaccurate. A new law is then proposed to explain the new results, for example, Sir Newton's theory of mechanics [6] was accepted for more than 200 years, until the beginning of the 20th century, however, experiments on objects moving at almost the speed of light could not be explained by Newton's theory. A new theory, the theory of relativity, was devised by Albert Einstein to explain these new results.

Most physical laws are stated mathematically. Mathematics is a very important and powerful tool for a physicist. Many experiments in physics involve measurements. The measurements give number that can be treated mathematically.

Nowadays it is difficult to divide physics into separate branches. This is because more and more **overlapping** areas of the different branches are being discovered. However, for convenience, physics is still divided into mechanics, heat, light, sound, electricity and magnetism, and **solid state physics**. There are also branches that cover **atomic, nuclear, and particle** physics. [7]

Mechanics is the study of material bodies and the forces that act on them. It is divided into two main branches: statics and dynamics. Statics is the study of forces acting on a body at rest, such as forces acting on a bridge. Dynamics is the study of forces that cause bodies to move, such as the forces acting on a swinging pendulum.

Heat studies are concerned with the effect of temperature on various substances. Heat is a form of energy. It can be changed into different forms of energy such as mechanical or electrical energy. Thermodynamics is the branch of "heat physics" that is the study of the transformation of energy.

The study of light is called **optics**. It investigates the nature and properties of light. An important part of optics is the study of optical instruments such as telescopes and microscopes.

Sound is studied in a branch of physics called **acoustics**. Acoustics is the study of properties of sound such as the ways in which sound is transmitted through air and other materials, and how sound is produced. An important part of acoustics is the design of acoustical buildings such as concert halls, and acoustical equipment.

Electricity and magnetism were once considered to be two separate subjects. During the 1800s, however, several connections were discovered between them. Electricity and magnetism are now studied as a single subject. The study of the connections between electricity and magnetism is called **electromagnetism**.

Solid state physics is a recent branch of physics. It explains the properties of a solid in terms of its atoms. One of the results of solid state physics has been the invention of the transistor. Transistors are now used in many different electronic devices.

Atomic, nuclear, and particle physics are also recent branches of physics. Atomic and nuclear physics include the study of the atom and the nucleus. Particle physics is the study of the particles that make up the nucleus and other subatomic particles. The mathematics needed for these subjects is very advanced. Many of the properties of atoms, nuclei, and particles are explained by **quantum theory**.

Notes

[1] ... we find the land surveyors of these people re-establishing vanishing landmarks and boundaries by utilizing the truths of geometry.

上句中，find 的意思是"发现"，后接宾语 the land surveyors of these people, re-establishing 引导的分词短语作宾语补足语，即 find sb. doing sth. 结构。

这句话可翻译成：……我们发现，这些民族的土地测量者利用几何知识重新确定消失了的土地标志和边界。

[2] A study of geometry and trigonometry is an essential part of the

training of the successful engineer, scientist, architect, and draftsman.

上句话列举出了许多行业，用于旁证几何学和三角学在生活中的重要性。

[3] Its history began in the 17th century when Newton, Leibniz and Bernoulli solved some simple differential equations arising from problems in geometry and mechanics.

上句揭示了微分方程的起源，提到几位伟大的数学家，其中牛顿(Sir Isaac Newton, 1642—1727)是英国物理学家、天文学家、数学家和哲学家，生于林肯郡。莱布尼茨(Gottfried Wilhelm von Leibniz, 1646—1716)是德国自然科学家、数学家和哲学家。伯努利(Jakob Bernoulli,即Jacques Bernoulli, 1654—1705)，瑞士数学家，变分法创始人之一，曾和莱布尼茨共同获得微积分学中的不少结果，对常微分方程的积分法有贡献，也是概率论的早期研究者，提出了关于大数法则的伯努利定理及伯努利数。关于微积分创立的优先权，在数学史上曾掀起了一场激烈的争论。实际上，牛顿在微积分方面的研究虽早于莱布尼茨，但莱布尼茨成果的发表则早于牛顿。目前，科学界普遍认为莱布尼茨和牛顿共同将积分和微分真正沟通起来，明确找到了两者内在的直接联系：微分和积分是互逆的两种运算，而这正是微积分建立的关键所在。因此，微积分是牛顿和莱布尼茨大体上完成的。

[4] For a long period of the history of mathematics, the centric place of mathematical methods was occupied by the logical deductions.

上句翻译成主动式较为符合中文的习惯：在数学史很长的时期内，逻辑推理一直占据数学方法的中心地位。

[5] In our times, computation is not only used to deal with a lot of information and data, but also to carry out some work that merely could be done earlier by logical deductions, for example, the proof of most of geometrical theorems.

上句可以译为：现在，计算不仅用来处理信息与数据，而且用来完成一些在以前只能靠逻辑推理来做的工作，例如证明几何定理。

[6] Sir Newton's theory of mechanics   牛顿力学体系

Sir Isaac Newton was an English physicist, mathematician, astronomer, natural philosopher, alchemist and theologian. His *Philosophiae Naturalis Principia Mathematica* published in 1687, is considered to be the most influential book in the history of science.

In this work, Newton described universal gravitation and the three laws of motion, laying the groundwork for classical mechanics, which dominated the scientific view of the physical universe for the next three centuries and is the basis for modern engineering. Newton showed that the motions of objects on Earth and of celestial bodies are governed by the same set of natural laws by demonstrating the consistency between Kepler's laws of planetary motion and his theory of gravitation, thus removing the last doubts about heliocentricism and advancing the scientific revolution.

[7] However, for convenience, physics is still divided into mechanics, heat, light, sound, electricity and magnetism, and solid state physics. There are also branches that cover atomic, nuclear, and particle physics.

上句基本概括了目前物理学的各个分支,可译成:然而,物理学仍旧可以分为力学、热学、光学、声学、电学和磁学,以及固态物理学。还有一些分支包括了原子物理学、核物理学和粒子物理学。

Key words and phrases

military	军事的；军用的
geometry	几何学
trigonometry	三角学
algebra	代数学
constant	常量
variable quantity	变量
calculus	微积分学
differential	微分的
proposition	命题
axiom	公理
postulate	假设，假定
theorem	定理
notation	符号
deduction	推论，演绎
computation	计算，估算
theory of mechanics	力学论
overlap	重叠，交叠
solid state physics	固态物理学
atomic	原子的
nuclear	核的；(原子)核的，核子的
particle	粒子，质点
thermodynamics	热力学
optics	光学
acoustics	声学
electromagnetism	电磁学
quantum theory	量子理论

Exercises

1. Oral practice.

(1) Why do we study mathematics and physics?
(2) What are the branches of mathematics?
(3) What branches of study is physics divided into?
(4) What do the three motion laws mention about?
(5) What causes body acceleration?

2. Fill in the blanks according to the above passages.

(1) Mathematics comes from man's social practice, for example, industrial and _____ production, commercial activities, military operations and scientific and _____ researches.
(2) Physics is the study of the properties of _____ and _____.
(3) _____ are a special and powerful tool of mathematics and are used to express conceptions and _____ very often.
(4) The conclusions in mathematics are obtained mainly by logical _____ and _____.
(5) Mechanics is the study of material bodies and the _____ that act on them.
(6) The rapid development of industry in the 17th century promoted the progress of _____ and technology and required dealing with variable _____.
(7) The study of the connections between electricity and magnetism is called _____.
(8) Acoustics is the study of properties of _____ such as the ways in which sound is _____ through air and other materials, and how sound is _____.

(9) An important part of _____ is the study of optical instruments such as telescopes and microscopes.

(10) Atomic and nuclear physics include the study of the _____ and the _____. Particle physics is the study of the _____ that make up the nucleus and other subatomic particles.

3. Judge whether the following statements are true or false, and correct the mistakes in the false statements.

(1) Physics studies all the properties of solid materials. ( )
Modification:

(2) Mechanics is divided into three main branches: statics mechanics, dynamics mechanics and electricity-magnetism mechanics. ( )
Modification:

(3) Heat can be changed into different forms of energy such as mechanical or electrical energy. ( )
Modification:

(4) The speed of sound in free space is 3×10^8 m/s. ( )
Modification:

(5) Electromagnetism studies the connections between electricity and magnetism. ( )
Modification:

(6) To deal with known numbers and some more complex practical problems, man established and then solved equation with algebra. ( )
Modification:

4. Translate the following technological phrases into English or Chinese.

(1) 数学 (2) 高等代数

(3) 微分方程 (4) 解析几何
(5) 逻辑推理 (6) 几何定理
(7) physical laws (8) the established law
(9) the law of conservation of energy
(10) Newton's theory of mechanics

5. Make sentences using the following phrases.

(1) play a role in
(2) belong to
(3) deal with
(4) carry out

*6. Read the following essay and answer the questions.

In mathematics, the Pythagorean theorem (American English) or Pythagoras' theorem (British English) is a relation in Euclidean geometry among the three sides of a right triangle. The theorem is named after the Greek mathematician Pythagoras, who by tradition is credited with its discovery and proof although knowledge of the theorem almost certainly predates him. The theorem is as follows:

In any right triangle, the area of the square whose side is the hypotenuse (the side opposite the right angle) is equal to the sum of the areas of the squares whose sides are the two legs (the two sides that meet at a right angle) as the below figure shown.

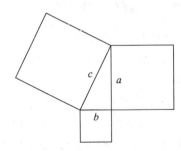

This is usually summarized as follows:

The square of the hypotenuse of a right triangle is equal to the sum of the squares on the other two sides.

Now, prove the Pythagorean theorem in English, in any way.

Pythagoras (580? BC – 500? BC): Greek philosopher and mathematician who founded in southern Italy a school that emphasized the study of musical harmony and geometry. He proved the universal validity of the Pythagorean theorem and is considered the first true mathematician.

Extended reading

Passage C

Mechanics

Mechanics is the study of forces and how they affect bodies. It is concerned with such things as the flight of airplanes, stresses on bridges, and the motion of engines.

Classical mechanics is divided into a number of branches. The action of forces on solid bodies is studied in dynamics and statics. Dynamics is concerned with forces that cause bodies to move. Statics is the study of forces acting on bodies that are at rest or moving with constant velocity. Another branch of mechanics is called **fluid dynamics**. Fluid mechanics is divided into several branches, including **hydrodynamics**, **hydrostatics**, and **aerodynamics**. Hydrodynamics is the study of the motion of a fluid under a force. Hydrostatics is the study of fluids at rest. Aerodynamics is the study of the effects of air on aircraft and missiles.

The basic laws of classical mechanics were studied about 300 years ago by Galileo and Sir Isaac Newton. These ideas remained unchanged until last century. Then Albert Einstein produced his theory of relativity. His theory changed the study of mechanics. However, the older mechanics of Newton and Galileo is still used today. In normal situations it is still very accurate.

Dynamics   Dynamics is the branch of physics that is the study of movement. There are three very important laws in dynamics. They are called Newton's laws of motion, after the times of Sir Isaac Newton. He was a very great English physicist who lived more than 300 years ago. He was the first person to codify these laws.

The first law of motion   An object usually stays where it is. It only moves if a force acts on it. When a lax object is moving it has a velocity. This velocity will only change if a force acts on the body. Imagine you are pushing a roller along a level piece of ground, if you stop rolling, the roller slows down and stops. This is because of the force of **friction** that acts between the roller and the ground. So you must keep pushing the roller to keep it moving. You have to push with enough force to overcome the friction force. If you push the roller harder, you increase the force, therefore its velocity increases.

The second law of motion   When a body speeds up or slows down, it **accelerates**. Acceleration is the rate of change of velocity. Suppose a body's velocity increase by two meters, every second. Then its acceleration is two meters per second. A force causes a body to accelerate. There is a simple relation between the size of the force acting on a body of constant mass and its acceleration. They are proportional to each other. If the force on a body is doubled, so is its acceleration. The acceleration also depends on the mass of the body. The larger the **mass**, the smaller the acceleration it will have for a particular force.

An example of this is when you hit a ball. When you do this you are putting a force on the ball. If you hit a ball twice as hard, it will go twice as far. Suppose the ball is twice as heavy, then you have to hit it twice as hard to make it go the same distance.

The third law of motion Every force creates a **reaction**. This reaction is as big as the force. It acts in the opposite direction. When your hand pushes on a table, the table is pushing back against your hand. Your pushing is called the **action** and the pushing up is the table's reaction. Without this reaction, your hand would push the table down. This does not seem like a law of motion, but it is. Without it, jet planes would not be able to fly. It is the reaction between the hot gases produced by the jet engine and the engine itself that pushes the aircraft forward.

■ Passage D

Function

Various fields of human have to do with relationships that exist between one **collection** of objects and another. Graphs, charts, curves, tables, formulas, and Gallup polls are familiar to everyone who reads the newspapers. These are merely devices for describing special relations in a quantitative fashion. Mathematicians refer to certain types of these relations as functions. In this section, we give an informal description of the function concept.

EXAMPLE 1. The force F necessary to stretch a steel **spring** a distance x beyond its natural length is proportional to x. That is, $F = -kx$, where k is a number independent of x called the spring constant. This formula, discovered by Robert Hooke in the mid-17th century, is called Hooke's law, and it is said to express the force as a function of the displacement.

EXAMPLE 2. The volume of a cube is a function of its edge-length. If the edges have length x, the volume V is given by the formula $V = x^3$.

EXAMPLE 3. A prime is any **integer** $n > 1$ that cannot be expressed in the form $n = ab$, where a and b are positive integers, both less than n. The first few primes are 2, 3, and 5, 7, 11, 13, 17, 19. For a given real number $x > 0$, it is possible to count the number of primes less than or equal to x. This number is said to be a function of x even though no simple algebraic formula is known for computing (without counting) when x is known.

The word "function" was introduced into mathematics by Leibniz, who used the term primarily to refer to certain kinds of mathematical formulas. It was later realized that Leibniz's idea of function was much too limited in its scope, and the meaning of the word has since undergone many stages of generalization. Today, the meaning of the function is essentially this: Given two sets, say X and Y, a function is a correspondence which associates with each element of X one and only one element of Y. The set X is called the **domain** of the function. Those elements of Y associated with the elements in X form a set called the **range** of the function. (This may be all of Y, but it need not be.)

Letters of the English and Greek **alphabets** are often used to denote functions. The particular letters f, g, h, F, G, H, and φ are frequently used for this purpose. If f is a given function and if x is an object of its domain, the notation $f(x)$ is used to designate that object in the range which is associated to x by the function f; and it is called the value of f at x or the image of x under f. The symbol $f(x)$ is read as "f of x".

Key words and phrases

dynamics	动力学
statics	静力学
fluid	流体
hydrodynamics	流体动力学,液体动力学
hydrostatics	流体静力学
aerodynamics	空气动力学,气体力学
friction	摩擦;摩擦力
accelerate	加速
mass	质量
reaction	反作用(力),反力;反应
action	作用(力)
collection	集合,聚集
spring	弹性,弹力
integer	整数
domain	定义域
range	值域
alphabet	字母表

Application writing

申请信
Letters of application

求职或求学,一般都要求有书面的申请。申请信是英语书信中最常见的。申请信要写得简明扼要,篇幅不宜太长,建议不超过一页。申请信要尽量反映自己的长处,以便给别人留下较深刻的印象,获得面试或录用的机会。申请信用词应比较规范,属于正式文体。申请信的语气要诚恳,态度要不卑不充。写信之前,如果有可能,要尽量弄清楚招聘人的姓名和职务,以便将申请信及简历直接寄给收信人本人,这样可避免延误,也便于以后查询。

1. 申请信的格式

申请信一般包括以下几个方面:

(1) 申请的目标和契机。

是申请读书还是应聘?是通过广告或别人介绍得知还是自我引荐试试机会?

(2) 本人的资格或所具备申请的条件。

申请信要介绍本人的基本情况,如年龄、实践经验等。如没有工作经验,可提及在学校的社会工作或者类似工作的经验,与求职有关的情况要着重说明。对自己的特长介绍要实事求是。

(3) 申请的动机或理由。

申请的动机和理由要令人信服。如果是想离开原单位,务必注意不要对原工作单位过分指责,也不要自贬或乞求。

(4) 本人的要求。

如果是申请去国外留学或进修,则与求职略有差别,可说明本国是否提供资助,是否希望获得奖学金,是否自费留学。如果要求提供勤工俭学机会,或要求对方提供住宿等,也可以在信中说明。

(5) 今后联系的方法、地址、时间及客套话。

如果申请或应聘比较重要的岗位职务,还要提供相关证明。

2. 申请信的示例

Mr. ×××

Chair, English Department

Guilin University of Electronic Technology, 541004

Guilin, China

Dear Mr. ×××,

  I am writing to you to apply for the position of instructor of English that is available at your University. There are many academic and professional merits that I have gained in the past five years as a teacher of both English and communication. These merits make me a suitable candidate for the position. I have also participated in many intercultural studies and possess a strong enthusiasm for immersing myself both personally and professionally in another culture. As I will explain further, these attributes prompted me to apply for this position.

During my assignment at the ×××University, I taught English courses to students of various cultural groups. This experience involved preparing lectures for literature discussions, writing instructions, and familiarizing my students to use in their course. I also gained valuable teaching knowledge through creating and developing various compositional tasks.

Through these various academic experience and endeavors I have gained knowledge and insight which has enriched my awareness of and fired my curiosity towards other cultures. As noted on my included transcript, I was enrolled in Intercultural Communication Course Hong Kong 2013. In this course training I gained a good knowledge of eastern cultures, which would aid my foreign oriental traveling. I feel that I am armed with a plethora of talents and awareness regarding both living and teaching in another quite different culture. Both my talents as a teacher and my personal attributes are well documented in the enclosed letters of recommendation.

Enclosed are the materials which you have requested, a research paper and my academic honors in writing. I hope to hear from you in the near future and wish to thank you very much for your time and consideration.

Sincerely yours

×××

Unit Two

Computer Science

Goals

After studying the unit, you should be able to

- understand the steps of software engineering process.
- distinguish top-down and object-oriented methodologies in problem-solving in your understanding.
- apply top-down design methodology to develop an algorithm to solve a problem.
- define the key terms in object-oriented design.
- understand the development background of virtualization technologies.
- describe what is a virtual machine and its application areas.
- learn the different versions of Windows operating systems.

 Texts

■ Passage A

Computer Problem Solving

The hardware of a computer can be turned on, but it does nothing without **programs** that make up the computer's software. It's crucial to understanding how software works in a modern computing system.

Computer can do nothing without being told what to do. A computer is not intelligent. A human (the programmer) must analyze the problem, develop the instructions for solving the problem, and then have the computer carry out the instructions.

There are three phases in the problem-solving process: **algorithm development phase, implementation phase, and maintenance phase**[1]. See Fig. 2-1. The output from the algorithm development phase is a plan for a general solution to the problem. The output from the second phase is a working computer program that implements the algorithm, that is, a specific solution to the problem. There is no output from the third phase, unless errors are detected or changes need to be made. If so, these errors or changes are sent back either to the first phase or second phase, whichever is appropriate. See Fig. 2-2.

Algorithm Development Phase	
Analyze	Understand (define) the problem.
Propose algorithm	Develop a logical sequence of steps to be used to solve the problem.
Test algorithm	Follow the steps as outlined to see if the solution truly solves the problem.
Algorithm Implementation Phase	
Code	Translate the algorithm (the general solution) into a programming language.
Test	Have the computer follow the instructions. Check the results and make corrections until the answers are correct.
Algorithm Maintenance Phase	
Use	Use the program.
Maintain	Modify the program to meet changing requirements or to correct any errors.

Fig. 2-1 Computer problem-solving process

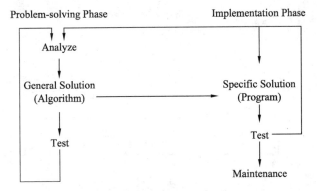

Fig. 2-2　Interaction between problem-solving phases

　　We must develop a methodology[2] that begins with the problem statement and hopefully ends with the plan, an algorithm, and then converting the algorithm into a program. There are two methodologies that are currently used: top-down design (also called functional decomposition)[3] and object-oriented design (OOD)[4]. We introduce top-down design first because it mirrors how we solve problems in general. We also cover object-oriented design, a newer methodology. In recent years OOD has become very popular in the computing world.

　　The top-down design process starts by breaking the problem into a set of subproblems. Then, each subproblem is divided into subproblems. This process continues until each subproblem is defined at a level basic enough so that further decomposition is not necessary. We are creating a hierarchical structure, also known as a tree structure, of problems and subproblems, called modules.

　　Let's apply this top-down design process to the pleasant task of planning a large party. There are two main tasks: inviting the people and preparing the food. The tree diagram in Fig. 2-3 shows the process we have broken down so far. Note that a module at each level expands a task or step at the level above.

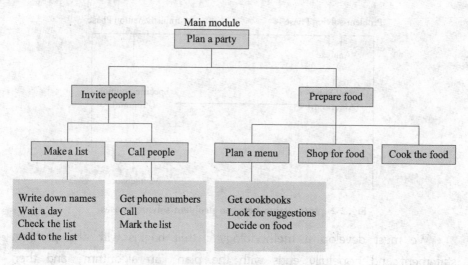

Fig. 2-3　Subdividing the party planning

　　Object-oriented design is a problem-solving methodology that produces a solution to a problem in terms of self-contained entities called **objects**, which are composed of both data and operations that manipulate the data. Object-oriented design focuses on the objects and their interactions within a problem.

　　Data and algorithms that manipulate the data and bundled together in the object-oriented view, thus making each object responsible for its own manipulation (behavior). Object-oriented problem solving involves isolating the **classes** within the problem. Objects communicate with each other by sending messages (invoking each other's methods). A class contains **fields** that represent the properties and behaviors of the class. A field can contain data value(s) and/or methods (subproblems). A **method** is a named algorithm that manipulates the data values in the object. A class in the general sense is a pattern for what an object looks like and how it behaves.

　　To summarize, top-down design methods focus on the process of transforming input into output, resulting in a hierarchy of tasks. Object-oriented design focuses on the data objects that are to be transformed, resulting in a hierarchy of objects. Read the specification of the software you want to build and underline the nouns and the verbs. The nouns become objects; the verbs become operations. In a top-down design, the verbs are the primary focus; in an object-oriented design, the nouns are the primary focus.

■ Passage B

Operating Systems and Virtual Machine

1. Introduction

With the increased development of applications, **operating systems** and the Internet, computer users more often face software incompatibility. Older applications that are important for users often do not work on newer computer systems as they do not support new hardware and new operating systems. Furthermore, programmers and application developers have to test their applications to work in different software environments. There is a need for **running** and testing applications on different software environments without a lot of reinstallation of the existing software. For this and lots of other purposes the best solution is **virtualization**. It is a method that allows installation of other operating systems inside the existing one. The operating system existing on a certain computer system is called a **host operating system** and a new **installed** operating system is called virtual. The tool used for installing virtual operating systems creates a virtual computer and a virtual operating system is installed on a virtual computer so it is not directly connected to hardware resources. This virtual computer in combination with the virtual operating system is called a virtual machine. A virtual computer has lower hardware resources than physical hardware since the tool for virtualization emulates older devices with lower performance than physical hardware. A virtual machine manages hardware resources through the host operating system. On the basis of this we can conclude that if a virtual machine runs on the identical hardware, but on different host operating systems, virtual machine performance is not identical for all host operating systems.

2. Virtualization

Nowadays virtualization is ubiquitous and virtualization technologies play an important role in many IT fields. The main advantages of virtualization in general are as follows: it can rapidly reduce cost and dangerousness of the experiments, portability of a virtual machine to another is simple, it has improved security, it enables parallelization, it decreases time expenses needed for administration of a large amount of desktops and workstations, etc.

The virtual machine is a technology that creates one or multiple virtual environments on a single physical machine. The virtual machines are isolated from each other and the underlying physical machine, and they give users the illusion of accessing a real machine directly. The virtual machine is a completely independent computer system and a virtual operating system needs regular updates and antivirus protection and it also has its own IP address. Virtual machines have been widely used in the following applications: × Server consolidation, × Intrusion and fault tolerance, × System migration, × Virtual appliance, × Debugging and testing. There are many ways to provide the virtualized environment. Virtualization layer or platform supports virtual environments with software approaches. It maps virtual requests from a virtual machine to physical requests. Virtualization can take place at several different levels of abstractions, including the ISA (Instruction Set Architecture), HAL (Hardware Abstraction Layer), operating system level and user level. ISA-level virtualization emulates the entire instruction set architecture of a virtual machine in software. HAL-level virtualization exploits the similarity between the architectures of the virtual and host machine, and directly executes certain instructions on the native CPU without emulation. Fig. 2-4 shows HAL-level virtualization used in our performance measurements.

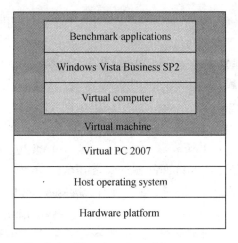

Fig. 2-4　The virtual machine concept

Operating system-level virtualization partitions the host operating system by redirecting I/O requests, system calls or library function calls. User-level virtualization is described in detail. Authors present a solution for portable Windows applications/customizations based on user-level virtualization technologies. Their solution compared with some existing solutions based on virtual machine technologies is more efficient in performance and storage capacity. Different levels of virtualization can differ in isolation strength, resource requirement, performance overhead, scalability and flexibility. In general, when the virtualization layer is closer to the hardware, the created virtual machines are better isolated from each other and better separated from the host machine, but with more resource requirements and less flexibility.

3. Windows operating systems

Windows operating systems are most widely used on desktop and portable computers. Every new version of Windows brings many new features and enhancements. When Windows XP was launched in 2001, it brought revolution to operating systems. It had a new graphical user interface with lots of visual effects, new features, improved performance, stability and security. To achieve better performance, Windows XP uses numerous techniques such as asynchronous I/O, optimized protocols for networks, kernel-based graphics and sophisticated caching of file-system data. When compared with Windows XP, Windows Vista presents a lot of new features and a new kernel. Almost every part of Windows Vista has some changes. Areas of Windows Vista that have major changes influencing performance are: processes and threads, I/O, memory management, power management, startup and shutdown, reliability and recovery, and security. A new CPU scheduling policy improves performance by bringing many enhancements in the area of processes and threads. Memory management includes numerous new technologies that improve performance like: SuperFetch, ReadyBoot, ReadyBoost, and ReadyDrive. SuperFetch logs user activities and preloads software into memory to reduce their load times. ReadyBoot analyzes the boot process and allocates additional random access memory to optimize the process. ReadyBoost uses a flash memory as a drive for system caching. ReadyDrive enables disk caching on hybrid hard disk flash memory to boot up faster, resume from hibernation in less time, and preserve battery power. Furthermore, other improvements include: new Multimedia Class Scheduler Service that supports glitch-free audio and video streaming, new display driver architecture called WDDM (Windows Display Driver Model) that gives users better performance, stability and security and DirectX 10 support. The underlying design goal for Windows 7 was performance improvement in key user scenarios with focus on user responsiveness. Windows 7 is built on the same core architecture as Windows Vista and therefore all features from Windows Vista are retained in Windows 7 and most of them are enhanced. ReadyBoost improvements include support for caching pagefile-backed pages, concurrent use of multiple flash devices and support for a 32-GB cache. ReadyBoot is improved by using compression and reducing memory footprint. Memory manager is improved by adding own working set to system cache, paged pool, and a pageable system code. Also, registry operations are enhanced by removing memory mapping. Improved DWM (Desktop Window

Manager) reduces memory footprint per window by 50%. Kernel Dispatcher Lock is replaced with several finer-grained synchronization techniques thus effectively distributing resource contention. UMS (User Mode Scheduling) improves performance by separating a user-mode thread and a kernel-mode thread. Scalability for applications that manage large amounts of memory is improved by removing the memory manager PFN (Physical Frame Number) global lock. DirectX 11 improves scalability and performance by introducing new features. Core Parking improves power efficiency by dynamically selecting a set of processors (sockets) that should stay idle and Windows 7 includes support up to 256 logical processors. The main benefit from a new kernel part of Windows 7 called MinWin is that it can be built, booted and tested separately from the rest of the system.

Notes

[1] algorithm development phase

算法开发阶段。在软件开发过程中,这个阶段完成软件的需求分析和设计工作。

algorithm implementation phase

算法实施阶段。在软件开发过程中,这个阶段完成软件的编码和测试工作。

algorithm maintenance phase

算法维护阶段。在软件开发过程中,维护阶段是最后的任务,也是软件的生命周期当中持续时间最长的阶段,是软件在交付客户使用之后对软件的错误、新的需求等进行的维护。

上面3个软件工程中的术语概括了软件开发的整个过程。

[2] methodology　方法学,研究法,一套方法

methodology 可指对一个学科的研究方法进行的理论分析,也可指一个学科特有的一整套方法与步骤。然而,近些年来,在科学、技术语境中,methodology 越来越多地被用作颇带炫耀夸张色彩的 method 的替换词。本文中的 methodology 也就是 method 的含义。

[3] top-down design (also called functional decomposition)

自上而下的设计,也可以叫作功能分解,将大的问题逐步细化求解。与此对应的还有自下而上的设计(bottom-up design),解决问题的过程是从细节开始考虑。两种方法各有利弊,软件设计的过程多数都是综合使用两种方法。

[4] object-oriented design (OOD)

面向对象设计。面向对象的思想是将数据和操作封装在"对象"这个实体当中,对象之间的交互是通过消息传递来实现的,对象维护自己的数据,并处理发给自己的消息。

Key words and phrases

program	程序
algorithm	算法
module	模块
object	对象(对象是类的实例)
class	类(类是对象的模板)
field	域(即对象的成员)
method	方法
operating system	操作系统
run	运行
virtualization	虚拟
host operating system	主机操作系统
install	安装
server consolidation	服务器整合
intrusion and fault tolerance	入侵容错系统
system migration	系统迁移
virtual appliance	虚拟应用
debugging and testing	调试和测试

Exercises

1. Oral practice.

(1) Top-down design is prevalent in the 20th century, and object-oriented design appeared and used from the 1990s. Please describe the difference between top-down design and object-oriented design according to your own understanding.

(2) Differentiate the terms "program" and "software" in English after the teacher's explanation.

(3) Decribe how different host operating systems influence virtual machine performance.

2. Fill in the blanks with the words or phrases given in the list below. Change the word form where necessary.

| so far | known as | focus on | note that | so that |
| start by | whichever | algorithm | subproblem | |

(1) _____ are the rhythms of computer science.

(2) These errors or changes are sent back either to the first phase or second phase, _____ is appropriate.

(3) The top-down design process _____ breaking the problem into a set of _____.

(4) This process continues until each subproblem is defined at a level basic enough _____ further decomposition is not necessary.

(5) We are creating a hierarchical structure, also _____ a tree

structure, of problems and subproblems, call modules.

(6) We have received no information _____.

(7) _____ a module at each level expands a task or step at the level above.

(8) Object-oriented design _____ the objects and their interactions within a problem.

3. Introduction and translation of specific expressions.

在科技英语中,要表达"如图所示"这个含义,有以下几个说法:
- See Fig. 2-1.
- ..., as shown in Fig. 2-1.
- As Fig. 2-1 shows, ...
- ... is shown in Fig. 2-1.

其中,能够用于表达此意的单词有 show, describe, represent, demonstrate, illustrate 等。

请完成下列句子的翻译:
(1) 企业内部网用户的安全性不再局限于防火墙内部,如图 2-1 所示。
(2) OSI 模型是国际标准化组织提供的网络参考模型,如图 2-1 所示。

4. Technological English writing.

(1) Write a top-down design for sorting a list of names into alphabetical order.

(2) Describe the advantages of a virtual machine.

Extended reading

■ Passage C

Programming Languages

In the von Neumann machine architecture[1], the CPU(Central Processing Unit) takes instructions one at a time and executes them. The instructions that a computer can execute directly are those that are built into the hardware. Recall that just as each lock has a specific key that opens it, each type of computer has a specific set of instructions, called the computer's machine language. However, instructions written in a programming language can be translated into the instructions executed directly.

Machine language is the initial language of computer. How are computer instructions represented? Since there are a finite number of instructions, the processor designers simply list the instructions and assign them a binary code. The relationship between the processor and instructions it can carry out is completely integrated. The electronics of the CPU inherently recognize the binary representations of the specific commands. Each machine-language instruction does only one very low-level task. In fact, very few programs are written in machine language today. Most are written in **high-level languages** and then translated into machine language.

And then we graduate to **assembly language**, which allows the programmer to use **mnemonics** to represent instructions rather than numbers. A program written in assembly language is input to the **assembler**, which translates the assembly-language instructions into the machine code. The machine code, the output from the assembler, is then executed. The hall-mark of an assembly language is that each assembly-language instruction is translated into one machine-language instruction.

Finally, we move up to a high-level language, which provides a richer set of instructions that makes the programmer's life even easier, the translation process is more difficult. Programs that translate programs written in a high-level language are called **compilers** [2]. In the early days, the output of a compiler was an assembly-language version, which then had to be run through an assembler to finally get the machine code. As computer scientists began to have a deeper understanding of the translation process, compilers became more sophisticated and the assembly-language phase was often eliminated. A program written in a high-level language can be run on any computer that has an appropriate compiler for the language.

An interpreter [3] is a translating program that translates and executes the statements in sequence. Unlike an assembler or compiler that produces machine code as output, which is then executed in a separate step, an interpreter translates a statement and then immediately executes it. An interpreter can be viewed as simulators for the language in which a program is written. Both a translator and a simulator accept programs in a high-level language as input. The translator simply produces an equivalent program in the appropriate machine language. The simulator executes the input program directly.

High-level languages came in two varieties: those that were compiled and those that were interpreted. FORTRAN, COBOL, PASCAL, C and C^{++} were compiled; BASIC and LISP were interpreted. Because of the complexity of the software interpreters, programs in interpreted languages usually ran much more slowly than compiled programs. As a result, the trend was towards compiled languages until the advent of Java.

Java was introduced in 1996 and took the computing community by storm. In the design of Java, portability was of primary importance. To achieve optimum portability, Java is compiled into a standard machine language called bytecode. How can a standard machine language run? A software interpreter called the JVM (Java Virtual Machine) takes the bytecode program and executes it. That is, bytecode is not the machine language for any particular hardware processor. Any machine that has a JVM can run the compiled Java program.

Microsoft has developed a language called C# (pronounced "C sharp") designed to compete directly with Java. Things happen so rapidly in the world of computing.

At each stage of the development of programming languages, the languages themselves become more abstract; that is, they allow us to express more and more complex processing with one statement. As you might expect, this move from the concrete to the abstract mirrors the history of software development.

A programming language is an artificial language that made up of symbols, special words and a set of rules, used to construct a program, that is, to express a meaningful sequence of instructions for a computer. It comes in many forms and many levels of complexity, but all are made up of two parts: **syntax**, the part that says how the instructions of the language can be put together, and **semantics**, the part that says what the instructions mean.

Notes

[1] von Neumann machine architecture

冯·诺依曼式计算机体系结构。冯·诺依曼理论的要点是:数字计算机的数制采用二进制;计算机应该按照程序逐条执行指令。为了完成上述功能,计算机必须具备五大基本组成部件,包括输入数据和程序的输入设备、记忆程序和数据的存储器、完成数据加工处理的运算器、控制程序执行的控制器和输出处理结果的输出设备。从第一台数字电子计算机 ENIAC 到当前最先进的计算机都采用的是冯·诺依曼体系结构,所以冯·诺依曼被称为"数字计算机之父"。

[2] compiler

编译程序。它把高级语言(如 FORTRAN, COBOL, PASCAL, C 等)源程序作为输入,进行翻译转换,产生出机器语言的目标程序,然后再让计算机去执行这个目标程序,得到计算结果。编译程序工作时,先进行词法分析和语法分析;然后进行代码优化,存储分配和代码生成。为了完成这些任务,编译程序采用对源程序进行多次扫描的办法,每次扫描集中完成一项或几项任务,也有一项任务分散到几次扫描去完成的。

[3] interpreter

解释程序,是高级语言翻译程序的一种,它将源语言(如 BASIC)书写的源程序作为输入,解释一句后就提交计算机执行一句,并不形成目标程序。就像外语翻译中的"口译"一样,说一句翻一句,不产生全文的翻译文本。这种工作方式非常适合人通过终端设备与计算机会话,如在终端上打一条命令或语句,解释程序就立即将此语句解释成一条或几条指令,提交硬件立即执行,并且将执行结果反映到终端。解释程序执行速度很慢是它固有的缺陷,例如源程序中出现循环解释程序会重复地解释并提交执行循环体的一组语句,造成很大浪费。

Key words and phrases

machine language	机器语言
high-level language	高级语言
assembly language	汇编语言
mnemonic	助记符号(指帮助记忆一些较长或复杂指令的名称或缩写符号)
assembler	汇编程序
compiler	编译程序
interpreter	解释程序
bytecode	字节码文件
syntax	语法(指构造语言表达式或句法的文化规则)
semantics	语义;语义学

■ **Passage D**

Computer Graphics

The use of computer graphics pervades many diverse fields. Applications range from the production of charts and graphs, to the generation of realistic images for television and motion pictures to the interactive design of mechanical parts. To encompass all these uses, we can adopt a simple definition: Computer graphics is concerned with all aspects of using a computer to generate images. We can classify applications of computer graphics into four main areas:
- Display of information
- Design

- Simulation
- User interfaces

1. Display of information

Graphics has always been associated with the display of information. Examples of the use of **orthographic projections** to display floorplans of buildings can be found on 4000-year-old Babylonian stone tablets. Medical imaging uses computer graphics in a number of exciting ways.

2. Design

Professions such as engineering and architecture are concerned with design. Although their applications vary, most designers face similar difficulties and use similar methodologies. One of the principal characteristics of most design problems is the lack of a unique solution. Hence, the designer will examine a potential design and then will modify it, possibly many times, in an attempt to achieve a better solution. Computer graphics has become an indispensable element in this iterative process.

3. Simulation

Some of the most impressive and familiar uses of computer graphics can be classified as simulations. Video games demonstrate both the visual appeal of computer graphics and our ability to generate complex imagery in real time. The insides of an arcade game reveal state-of-the-art hardware and software. Computer-generated images are also the heart of flight simulators, which have become the standard method for training pilots. The savings in dollars and lives realized from use of these simulators has been enormous. The computer-generated images (which) we see on television and in movies have advanced to the point that they are almost indistinguishable from real-world images.

4. User interfaces

The interface between the human and the computer has been radically altered by the use of computer graphics. Consider the electronic office. The figures were produced through just such an interface. A secretary sits at a workstation, rather than at a desk equipped with a typewriter. This user has a pointing device, such as a mouse, that allows him to communicate with the workstation. The display consists of a number of icons that represent the various operations the secretary can perform. For example, there might be an icon of a mailbox that, if pointed to and clicked on, causes any electronic-mail messages to appear on the screen.

The most common type of graphics monitor employing a **CRT** (**cathode ray tube**) is the **raster-scan display**, based on television technology. In a raster-scan system, the electron beam is swept across the screen, one row at a time from top to bottom. As the electron beam moves across each row, the beam intensity is turned on and off to create a pattern of illuminated spots.

Picture definition is stored in a memory area called the refresh buffer or **frame buffer**. This memory area holds the intensity values for all the screen points. Stored intensity values are then retrieved from the frame buffer and "painted" on the screen one row (scan line) at a time. Each screen point is referred to as a **pixel** or pel (shortened forms of picture element). The capability of a raster-scan system to store intensity information for each screen point makes it well suited for the realistic display of scenes containing subtle shading and color patterns. Home television sets and printers are examples of other systems using raster-scan methods.

When operated as a **random-scan display** unit, a CRT has the electron beam directed only to the parts of the screen where a picture is to be drawn. Random-scan monitors draw a picture one line at a time and for this reason are also referred to as a **vector** display (or stroke-writing or calligraphic display). The component lines of a picture can be drawn and refreshed by a random-scan system in any specified order. A pen plotter operates in a similar way and is an example of a random-scan, **hard-copy device**.

An alternative method for maintaining a screen image is to store the picture information inside the CRT instead of refreshing the screen. A **direct-view storage tube** (**DVST**) stores the picture information as a charge distribution just behind the phosphor-coated screen. Two electron guns are used in a DVST. One, the primary gun, is used to store the picture pattern; the other, the flood gun, maintains the picture display.

The term **flat-panel display** refers to a class of video devices that have reduced volume, weight, and power requirements compared with a CRT. A significant feature of flat-panel displays is that they are thinner than CRTs, and we can hang them on walls or wear them on our wrists. Since we can even write on some flat-panel displays, they will soon be available as pocket notepads.

Current uses for flat-panel displays include small TV monitors, calculators, pocket video games, laptop computers, armrest viewing of movies on airlines, advertisement boards in elevators, and graphics displays in applications requiring rugged, portable monitors.

Typically, graphics programming packages provide functions to describe a scene in terms of these basic geometric structures, referred to as **output primitives**, and to group sets of output primitives into more complex structures. Each output primitive is specified with input coordinate data and other information about the way that the object is to be displayed. Points and straight-line segments are the simplest geometric components of pictures. Additional output primitives that can be used to construct a picture include circles and other conic sections, quadric surfaces, spline curves and surfaces, polygon color areas, and character strings.

Some typical applications of computer-generated animation are entertainment (motion pictures and cartoons), advertising, scientific and engineering studies, and training and education. Although we tend to think of animation as implying object motions, the term computer animation generally refers to any time sequence of visual changes in a scene. In addition to changing object position with translations or rotations, a computer-generated animation could display time variations in object size, color, transparency, or surface texture.

Some steps in the development of an animation sequence are well suited to computer solution. These include object manipulations and rendering, camera motions, and the generation of in-betweens. Animation packages, such as Wave-front, for example, provide special functions for designing the animation and processing individual objects.

Key words and phrases

orthographic projection	八面图形投影法
CRT(cathode ray tube)	阴极射线管
raster-scan display	光栅扫描显示器
frame buffer	帧缓冲器
pixel (pel)	像素
random-scan display	随机扫描显示器;随机扫描显示
vector	矢量,向量
hard-copy device	硬拷贝设备
DVST(direct-view storage tube)	直视存储管
flat-panel display	平板显示器;平板显示
output primitive	输出图元

Application writing

如何撰写科技论文摘要

How to write an abstract of scientific papers

I have the strong impression that scientific communication is being seriously hindered by poor quality abstracts.

—Sheila M. McNab

  摘要也称为内容提要。根据美国国家标准定义(ASNI 239.14,1979),摘要是"一篇精确代表文献内容的简短文字"。在英语科技论文中,摘要是为了方便学术交流,摘要常常被专业期刊文献杂志编入索引资料或者文献刊物,如美国的 SCI,EI,CA 等。阅读科技文章时,绝大多数人首先阅读的是论文的摘要,然后才进行进一步的阅读。

  科技论文摘要是原文内容要点的具体总结,包括目的、方法、论文所设计的范围、提供结果或者创新、做出结论或对下一步的工作提出建议。

  科技论文着重讲述客观现象和科技真理,所以与日常英语和文学著作相比,被动语态的使用要广泛得多。被动句在科技英语中约占 1/3,比文艺类作品高出十几倍。英文摘要更是如此。汉语中被动句用得少,且可以使用没有行为主体的无人称句,而这时在英语中就要使用被动句了。在摘要中,几乎没有使用第一人称单数(I)的。

  示例:

Abstract

The trend of the wireless communication system is to provide various types of services such as voice, data and video, etc. Due to the limited radio resources with international agreement, how to achieve the optimum system capacity becomes a paramount issue. In this paper, the idea of channel partitioning (CP) employing different reuse factors is used to support multiple services that require different signal-to-interference ratios (SIRs) in cellular systems. Two types of service are considered in this paper. Thus, a large reuse factor is used to support high SIR required service while a small reuse factor is used to support low SIR required service.

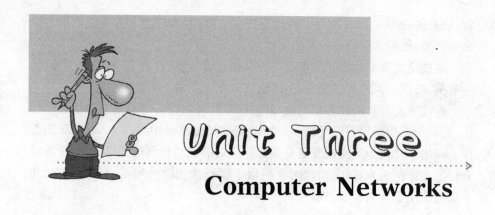

Unit Three
Computer Networks

Goals

After studying this unit, you should be able to
- explain various topologies of local-area networks.
- explain why network technologies are best implemented as open systems.
- explain packet switching.
- explain what is the Internet-of-things.

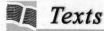 **Texts**

■ Passage A

Networking

For many years, computers have played as important a role in communication as they do in computation. This communication is accomplished by using computer networks. Like complex highway systems that connect roads in various ways to allow cars to travel from their origin to their destination, computer networks form an infrastructure that allows data to travel from some source computer to a destination.

Usually, the connections between computers in a network are made using physical wires or cables. However, some connections are **wireless**, using radio waves or infrared signals to convey data.

A key issue related to computer networks is the data transfer rate, the speed with which data is moved from one place on a network to another. Sometimes the data transfer rate is referred to as the bandwidth of a network.

Another key issue in computer networks is the **protocols** that are used. A protocol is a set of rules describing how two things interact. Computer networks have opened up an entire frontier in the world of computing called the client/server model[1]. No longer do you think of computers solely in terms of the capabilities of the machine sitting in front of you, software systems are often distributed across a network, in which a client sends a request to a server for information or action, and the server responds.

Computer networks can be classified in various ways. A **local-area network(LAN)** connects a relatively small number of machines in a relatively close geographical area. A **wide-area network(WAN)** connects two or more local-area networks over a potentially large geographic distance. A wide-area network permits communication among smaller networks. Often one particular node on a LAN is set up to serve as a gateway to handle all communication going between that LAN and other networks.

Various configurations, called **topologies**[2], have been used to administer LANs.
- A **ring topology** connects all nodes in a closed loop on which messages travel in one direction. The nodes of a ring network pass along messages until they reach their destination.
- A **star topology** centers around one node to which all others are connected and through which all messages are sent. A star network puts a huge burden on the central node.
- In a **bus topology**, all nodes are connected to a single communication

line that carries messages in both directions. The nodes on the bus check any message sent on the bus, but ignore any that are not addressed to them.

These topologies are pictured in Fig. 3-1.

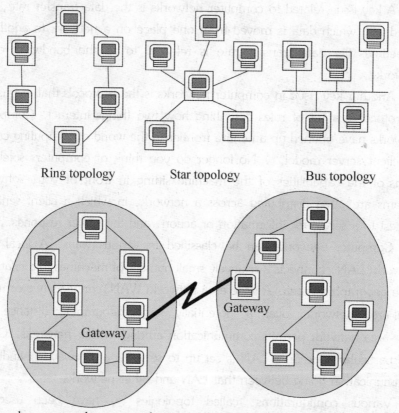

Fig. 3-1 Various network topologies

Communication between networks is called internetworking. The Internet, as we know it today, is essentially the ultimate wide-area network, spanning the entire globe. The Internet is a vast collection of smaller networks that have all agreed to communicate using the same protocols and to pass along messages so that they can reach their final destinations.

To improve the efficiency of transferring information over a shared communication line, messages are divided into fixed-sized packets. The packets are sent over the network individually to their destination, where they are collected and reassembled into the original message. This approach is referred to as packet switching[3].

The packets of a message may take different routes on their way to the final destination. Therefore, they may arrive in a different order than the way they were sent. The packets must be put into the proper order once again, and then combined to form the original message. This process is shown in Fig. 3-2.

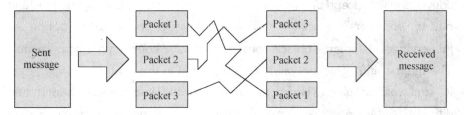

Fig. 3-2 Messages sent by packet switching

A packet of a message may make several intermediate hops between computers on various networks before it reaches its final destination. Network devices called **routers** are used to direct packets between networks. Intermediate routers don't plan out the packet's entire course; each router merely knows the best next step to get it closer to its destination. Eventually a message reaches a router that knows where the destination machine is. If a path is blocked due to a down machine, or if a path currently has a lot of network traffic, a router might send a packet along an alternative route.

Network connections have taken hobbyists to new levels. An activity that's growing in popularity is the GPS treasure hunt. GPS stands for Global Positioning System[4], which uses satellite technology to pinpoint your location within 25 feet. This is the technology that direction systems are used in cars to determine directions ("turn right at the next intersection").

Passage B

The Internet-of-Things

It is predictable that, within the next decade, the Internet will exist as a seamless fabric of classic networks and networked objects. Content and services will be all around us, always available, paving the way to new applications, enabling new ways of working, new ways of interacting, new ways of entertainment, and new ways of living. In such a perspective, the conventional concept of the Internet as an infrastructure network reaching out to end-users' terminals will fade, leaving space to a notion of interconnected "smart" objects forming pervasive computing environments. The Internet infrastructure will not disappear. On the contrary, it will retain its vital role as global backbone for worldwide information sharing and diffusion, interconnecting physical objects with computing/communication capabilities across a wide range of services and technologies.

This innovation will be enabled by the embedding of electronics into everyday physical objects, making them "smart" and letting them seamlessly integrate within the global resulting cyber physical infrastructure. This will give rise to new opportunities for the Information and Communication Technologies (ICT) sector, paving the way to new services and applications able to leverage the interconnection of physical and virtual realms.

Within such perspective, the term "the Internet-of-Things" (IOT) is broadly used to refer to the following: (i) the resulting global network interconnecting smart objects by means of extended Internet technologies, (ii) the set of supporting technologies necessary to realize such a vision (including, e. g. , RFIDs, sensor/actuators, machine-to-machine communication devices, etc.) and (iii) the ensemble of applications and services leveraging such technologies to open new business and market opportunities.

The Internet-of-Things is emerging as one of the major trends shaping the development of technologies in the ICT sector at large. The shift from an Internet used for interconnecting end-user devices to an Internet used for interconnecting physical objects that communicate with each other and/or with humans in order to offer a given service encompasses the need to rethink anew some of the conventional approaches customarily used in networking, computing and service provisioning/management.

From a conceptual standpoint, the IOT builds on three pillars, related to the ability of smart objects to: (i) be identifiable (anything identifies itself), (ii) to communicate (anything communicates) and (iii) to interact (anything interacts)—either among themselves, building networks of interconnected objects, or with end-users or other entities in the network. Developing technologies and solutions for enabling such a vision is the main challenge ahead of us.

At the single component level, the IOT will be based on the notion of "smart objects", or, simply, "things", which will complement the existing entities in the Internet domain (hosts, terminals, routers, etc.). We define smart objects (or things) as entities that:

● Have a physical embodiment and a set of associated physical features (e.g., size, shape, etc.).

● Have a minimal set of communication functionalities, such as the ability to be discovered and to accept incoming messages and reply to them.

● Possess a unique identifier.

● Are associated to at least one name and one address. The name is a human-readable description of the object and can be used for reasoning purposes. The address is a machine-readable string that can be used to communicate to the object.

● Possess some basic computing capabilities. This can range from the ability to match an incoming message to a given footprint (as in passive RFIDs) to the ability of performing rather complex computations, including service discovery and network management tasks.

● May possess means to sense physical phenomena (e.g.,

temperature, light, electromagnetic radiation level) or to trigger actions having an effect on the physical reality (actuators).

The last point in the definition above is the key one, and differentiates smart objects from entities traditionally considered in networked systems. In particular, the proposed classification includes devices considered in RFID research as well as those considered in wireless sensor networks (WSNs) and sensor/actor networks (SANETs).

The inclusion of such entities into a global networked system questions the architectural and algorithmic principles at the basis of the design of the Internet as we know it. In particular, the increased level of heterogeneity, due to the inclusion of devices with only very basic communication and computing capabilities, challenges the assumption that any device presents a full protocol stack, as well as the application of the end-to-end principle in network operations. From the conceptual standpoint, indeed, IOT is about entities acting as providers and/or consumers of data related to the physical world. The focus is on data and information rather than on point-to-point communications. This fact could push towards the adoption of recently proposed content-centric network architectures and principles, as will be discussed in the following sections.

From a system-level perspective, the Internet-of-Things can be looked at as a highly dynamic and radically distributed networked system, composed of a very large number of smart objects producing and consuming information. The ability to interface with the physical realm is achieved through the presence of devices able to sense physical phenomena and translate them into a stream of information data (thereby providing information on the current context and/or environment), as well as through the presence of devices able to trigger actions having an impact on the physical realm (through suitable actuators). As scalability is expected to become a major issue due to the extremely large scale of the resulting system, and considering also the high level of dynamism in the network (as smart objects can move and create *ad hoc* connections with nearby ones following unpredictable patterns), the quest for inclusion of self-management and autonomic capabilities is expected to become a major driver in the development of a set of enabling solutions.

From a service-level perspective, the main issues relate to how to integrate (or compose) the functionalities and/or resources provided by smart objects (in many cases in forms of data streams generated) into services. This requires the definition of: (i) architectures and methods for "virtualizing" objects by creating a standardized representation of smart objects in the digital domain, able to hinder the heterogeneity of devices/resources and (ii) methods for seamlessly integrating and composing the resources/services of smart objects into value-added services for end users.

The Internet-of-Things vision provides a large set of opportunities to users, manufacturers and companies. In fact, IOT technologies will find wide applicability in many productive sectors including, e.g., environmental monitoring, health care, inventory and product management, workplace and home support, security and surveillance.

From a user point of view, the IOT will enable a large amount of new always-responsive services, which shall answer to users' needs and support them in everyday activities. The arising of IOT will provide a shift in service provisioning, moving from the current vision of always-on services, typical of the Web era, to always-responsive situated services, built and composed at run-time to respond to a specific need and able to account for the user's context. When a user has specific needs, it will make a request and an ad hoc application, automatically composed and deployed at run-time and tailored to the specific context the user is in, will satisfy them.

In particular, IOT will likely expand starting from identification technologies such as RFID (Radio Frequency Identification), which are already widely used in a number of applications. At the same time, in its development path, IOT will likely build on approaches introduced in a variety of relevant field, such as **wireless sensor networks** (as a means to collect contextual data) and service-oriented architectures (SOA) as the software architectural approach for expanding Web-based services through IOT capabilities.

The Internet-of-Things is unlikely to arise as a brand new class of systems. We envision an incremental development path, along which IOT technologies will be progressively employed to extend existing IOT systems/ applications, providing additional functionalities related to the ability of interacting with the physical realm. In this sense, we do believe it is worth analyzing which research fields, among the ones subject of investigation in the last years, can be more relevant (in terms of techniques/solutions introduced or lessons learned) in the IOT scenario. In terms of enabling technologies, a key issue for IOT is the development of appropriate means for identifying smart objects and enabling interactions with the environment. In this sense, key building blocks are expected to be represented by wireless sensor networking technologies and RFID.

Radio frequency identification devices and solutions can nowadays be considered a mainstream communication technology, with a number of massive deployments, in particular in the goods management and logistics sectors. RFID is expected to play a key role as enabling identification technology in IOT. At the same time, its integration with sensing technologies brings alongside a number of challenges and issues. RFID applications have been so far mainly thought for use within isolated, vertically integrated systems, used only for identification and/or tracking of objects embedded with an RFID tag. Their use as part of a larger system, where identification of an object is only a step of the work flow to be executed to provide a final service, has not been fully explored yet.

Notes

[1] client/server model

客户端/服务器模式,是软件系统体系结构的一种。这种模式将应用程序处理分成两部分:用户的桌面计算机充当客户端,将请求通过网络发送给服务器端,服务器端分别处理各客户端的请求,并将应答发送给客户端。提供服务的服务器和接受服务的客户端也有可能在同一台机器上。例如,在提供网页的服务器上执行浏览器浏览本机所提供的网页,这样这一台机器就同时扮演了服务器和客户端。

[2] topology

拓扑结构。所谓网络拓扑结构,就是网络中的多台计算机以何种方式来组织和交互,常用的有环形结构、星形结构、总线形结构等。

[3] packet switching

包交换也称分组交换。它是将用户传送的数据划分成一定长度的若干包,每个部分叫作一个分组。在每个分组的前面加上一个分组头,用以指明该分组发往何地址,然后由交换机根据每个分组的地址标志,将它们转发至目的地,这一过程称为分组交换。进行分组交换的通信网称为分组交换网。

从交换技术的发展历史来看,数据交换经历了电路交换、报文交换、分组交换和综合业务数字交换的发展过程。分组交换实质上是在"存储—转发"基础上发展起来的。它兼有电路交换和报文交换的优点。分组交换在线路上采用动态复用技术,传送按一定长度分割为许多小段的数据——分组。每个分组标识后,在一条物理线路上采用动态复用的技术,把来自用户端的数据暂存在交换机的存储器内,接着在网内转发。到达接收端,再去掉分组头,将各数据字段按顺序重新装配成完整的报文。分组交换比电路交换的电路利用率高,比报文交换的传输时延小,交互性好。

[4] Global Positioning System

全球定位系统。这是一个由覆盖全球的 24 颗卫星组成的卫星系统。这个系统可以保证在任意时刻、地球上任意一点都可以同时观测到 4 颗卫星,保证卫星可以采集到该观测点的经纬度和高度,以便实现导航、定位、授时等功能。这项技术可以用来引导飞机、船舶、车辆及个人安全、准确地沿着选定的路线,准时到达目的地。

Key words and phrases

wireless	无线的
protocol	协议
protocol stack	协议栈
local-area network(LAN)	局域网
wide-area network(WAN)	广域网
configuration	配置
topology	拓扑学
ring topology	环形拓扑结构
star topology	星形拓扑结构
bus topology	总线形拓扑结构
router	路由器
interoperability	互操作性
cyber	网络
pillar	支柱
ad hoc	〈拉〉临时安排的,特别的,专门的
wireless sensor network	无线传感器网络

Exercises

1. Oral practise.

(1) Explain why network technologies are best implemented as open systems.
(2) Explain what is the Internet-of-things.

2. Fill in the blanks with the words or phrases given in the list below. Change the word form where necessary.

facilitate	pillar	compatibility	emerge
configuration	interact	in one sense	productive
transfer	at large		

(1) How do you _____ data from a desktop PC to laptop?
(2) This complexity gave rise to automated network management systems that _____ with network elements to gain data.
(3) This software will be able to bring Office integration and _____ solutions to the mobile and embedded user.
(4) It is the standard software _____ for the PC in computer rooms.
(5) The new trade agreement should _____ more rapid economic growth.
(6) _____, everything is self-creating.
(7) I spent a very _____ hour in the library.
(8) From a conceptual standpoint, the Internet-of-things builds on three _____.
(9) The Internet-of-things is _____ as one of the major trends shaping the development of technologies in the _____.

3. Match the word or acronym (首字母缩略词) with the definition or in the appropriate blank.

LAN	gateway	broadband	smart objects
ICT sector	WAN	bus topology	RFID
wireless sensor	networks		

(1) The Internet is a(n) _____.
(2) _____ is a node that handles communication between its LAN and other networks.
(3) Ethernet uses _____.
(4) _____ is the network technologies that generally provide data transfer speeds greater than 128Kbps.
(5) In particular the proposed classification includes devices considered in _____ research as well as those considered in _____ and sensor/actor networks.
(6) At the single component, the Internet-of-things win be based on the notion of _____, which will complement the existing entities in Internet domain.

4. Introduction and translation of specific expressions.

In Unit 2 and Unit 3, we have learned two expressions for emphasizing:

Note that ...

Keep in mind that ...

在科技英语中,句子成分的强调有4种表达法:
- 采用强调句型"It is (was) ... that (which, who) ..."来强调主语、宾语、状语和状语从句:

It is the losses caused by friction that (which) we must try to overcome. 我们必须克服由摩擦引起的各种损耗。
- 采用助动词 do (does, did) 来强调谓语动词:

These methods do work. 这些方法确实可行。
- 采用形容词 very 来强调名词:

The alternating current is the *very* current that makes radio possible. 就是交流电使无线电成为可能。
- 倒装强调:

This attraction we call magnetism. 这种吸引力我们称为磁性。

请完成下列句子的翻译：
(1) 物体受热时,分子(molecules)的平均速度提高。
(2) 月球的确具有引力(gravity)。
(3) 就在我们闭合电路的那一瞬间,电流开始流动。
(4) 电使得许许多多的东西成为可能。

Extended reading

Passage C

Electronic Commerce

Globalization is a phenomenon that has led to the integration of regional economies, societies, and cultures through communication, transport and trade. It is closely linked with economic globalization that stands for the integration of national economies into the international economy through trade, foreign direct investment, capital flows, migration, the spread of technology and military presence. However, the phenomenon of globalization is usually driven by a combination of economic, technological, socio-cultural, political, and biological factors.

In the global marketplace, companies are finding that the old strategies of conducting commerce are becoming obsolete. The relentless forces impacting today's business environment are the power of the customer, global trade, Internet enablers, deregulation, emerging markets, rapidly diminishing product life cycles, cut-throat competition, etc. Increasing competition has led to the rapid development of new products and consequently, shortening of product life cycles. In the past, companies competed by selling standardized, mass-based products based on lowest cost and possessing standards of average quality and availability. Today customers expect rapid availability of products and services along with other characteristics like cost, quality, etc. Customers demand speed and self-service, ability to do their own product configuration, more integration of product and service, lower costs and high quality, and highly personalized relationships.

In today's international competitive environment, no enterprise can expect to build a product, process or competitive advantage without integrating their strategies with those of their business partners. In the past, what occurred inside the four walls of the business was of primary importance. In contrast, today an organization's ability to look outward to their channel alliances to gain access to sources of unique competencies and physical resources is the measure of success. E-commerce is a unique platform that enables global collaborative alliances.

The 21st century is the age of information. It is information rather than productive assets, materials or labor that constitutes the fundamental source of wealth. Information sharing is essential for learning required for deliberate change, particularly in dynamic environments. E-commerce promotes high quality information exchanges among channel partners.

E-commerce describes the manner in which transactions take place over networks, mostly the Internet. Kalakota and Whinston define e-commerce from following perspectives:

From a communication perspective, e-commerce is the delivery of information, products/services, or payments over telephone lines, computer networks, or any other electronic means.

From a business process perspective, e-commerce is the application of technology toward the automation of business transactions and work flow.

From a service perspective, e-commerce is a tool that addresses the desire of firms, consumers and management to cut service costs while improving the quality of goods and increasing the speed of service delivery.

From an online perspective, e-commerce provides the capability of buying and selling, products and information on the Internet and other online services.

It can be stated that e-commerce describes the process of buying and selling or exchanging of products, services, information and finances via computer networks including the Internet in order to automate business processes, streamline work flow, cut costs and enhance service delivery. Business-to-business e-commerce implies that both the sellers and buyers are business corporations, while business-to-consumer implies that the buyers are individual consumers.

Due to globalization market, economical, societal and technological factors are creating a highly competitive business environment in which customers are the focal point. These factors can change quickly, sometimes in an unpredictable manner. Therefore companies need to react frequently and quickly to both the problems and the opportunities resulting from this new business environment. Boyett and Boyett emphasize that in order to succeed in this dynamic world, companies must take not only traditional actions such as lowering cost and closing unprofitable facilities but also innovative activities such as customizing products, creating new products, or providing superb customer service. Many critical response activities are greatly facilitated by e-commerce. In some cases, e-commerce is the only solution to these business pressures.

E-commerce provides an example of what Downes and Mui term a "disruptive technology" and opens door to new strategic initiatives. The growing importance of e-commerce has led to the emergence to technological platforms such as Data Mining, Internet, Intranet, Extranet, Electronic Data Interchange (EDI), Enterprise Resource Planning (ERP), etc. Customer data accumulates daily in an ever-increasing quantity. Large companies such as retailers, PC makers and car manufacturers build large data warehouses to store such information. E-commerce enables data mining tools to get over the cumbersomeness of the traditional data collection processes. Data mining technology can generate new business opportunities by providing capabilities like automated prediction of trends and behaviors; and automated discovery of previously unknown patterns.

The Internet, Intranet and Extranet are the most popular platforms for e-commerce. Internet is a public and global communication network that provides direct connectivity to anyone over a local-area network (LAN). Intranet is a corporate LAN or wide-area network (WAN) that uses Internet technology and is secured behind a company's firewalls. It operates as a private network with limited access. Only authorized employees are allowed to access it. Extranet is used by the company in order to establish contacts with channel partners. Extranets provide secured connectivity between corporation Intranets and the Intranets of business partners, material suppliers, financial service providers, government and customers.

EDI is the most widely used method of e-commerce connectivity. It provides for the computer-to-computer exchange of business transactions, such as customer's orders, invoices and shipping notices. The critical importance of EDI is that the transacting companies can use Enterprise Business Systems (EBS) that run on different software and hardware systems. It standardizes the process of trading and tracking routine business documents, such as purchase orders, invoices, payments, shipping, manifests, and delivery schedules. EDI translates these documents into a globally understood business language and transmits them between trading partners using secure telecommunication links.

ERP is enterprise-wide application software that can provide a centralized repository of information for the massive amount of daily transactions. It integrates core business processes from planning to production, distribution and sales. However, early versions of ERP solution focused on the Internet-based groupware, so effective integration with e-commerce was not established. Modern ERP solutions like SAP's R/3 overcome this limitation.

Security is often cited as a major barrier in e-commerce. Prospective buyers are suspicious about sending credit card information over the web. Prospective sellers worry that hackers will compromise their systems. The National Computer Security Association (NCSA) has identified four cornerstones of secure e-commerce: authenticity, privacy, integrity and non-repudiation.

Authenticity makes sure that the sender of a message is the one who he/she claim to be. Privacy keeps the contents of the message secret and they are known only to the sender and receiver. Integrity makes sure that the contents of the message are not modified during transmission. Non-repudiation makes sure that the sender of a message cannot deny that the message was actually sent and the receiver cannot deny that the message was received. The major solutions to e-commerce security are Encryption, Digital Signatures, Secure Socket Layer (SSL) and Secure Electronic Transactions (SET) protocols, Firewalls and Virtual Private Networks. Direct marketing can be realized as long as they sell established brands and their home site is well known, as is the case with Dell Computer.

On the business-to-business side, e-commerce systems provide competitive advantages by increasing the bargaining power of buying organization, better coordination among channel partners and making greater information available about the business processes and demands across the whole supply chain. On the business-to-customer side, e-commerce improves the whole cycle of customer relations, i.e., the acquisition, enhancement, and retention of customers. E-commerce has noticeable impact on the payment systems. The most common payment method for business-to-business e-commerce is credit cards. The other noticeable additions to payment systems are: electronic fund transfer, electronic cash, electronic cheque, debit cards, smart cards and unified payment systems.

E-commerce is changing the way people are recruited, evaluated, promoted, and developed. The Intranets play a major role in this transformation. Open and distance learning (ODL) is exploding, providing opportunities that never existed before. E-commerce is playing a revolutionary role in development of study materials, providing logistics support and linking open universities in developing countries with developed ones.

It is clear that e-commerce has dynamically transformed the way business is conducted in the global marketplace. It has completely changed the basic interface between a company and its customers, and also has impacted the profit margins earned by companies throughout the entire value chain. The very nature of e-commerce technologies gives enterprises unprecedented capabilities to focus on the customers, enhancing all activities concerning customer acquisition, retention and services.

The future of e-commerce cannot be limited to national boundaries. A global e-commerce has become the new success mantra. It means access to larger markets, mobility, and flexibility to employ workers and manufacture products anywhere using a worldwide telecommuting workforce. While geographical market boundaries may be falling, global interest-based communities will spring up. These cyber-nations' interest or taste differences are as real as political boundaries. Online firms may gain access to these cyber-nations and to a specific segment of consumer groups on a worldwide scale. Thus, this global e-commerce will lead the path of future generations.

■ Passage D

Hacking

The phrase "computer hacker" has changed over the last fifty years. In the 1960s, hackers were perceived as skilled computer wizards whose curiosity would lead to technological advancements. Today, the term "hacker" has a more negative connotation and invokes the image of malicious kids who get a thrill from defacing websites or professional criminals who wreak havoc on the Net. These perceptions, however, fuelled by some of the media, are often far from the truth.

Although the term "hacker" still has both positive and negative connotation, hacking does not. Hacking refers to the trespassing or accessing of a website without authorization. Unauthorized entry can lead to legal consequences, particularly if a hacker is deliberately violating the website's right to privacy. The computer Fraud and Abuse Act states that purposefully entering a site without authority and intentionally accessing classified information is unlawful. Whether the hackers damage the content or leave the site untouched, their ability to infiltrate secure systems is powerful and disturbing. One study asserts that 59% of all company-owned websites were hacked during 1997.

In the famous *New York Times* hacking incident that occurred on September 13, 1998, hackers broke into the newspaper's website and replaced the page with pornographic material and a threatening message. Security breaches like this one have led companies such as Honeynet to design decoy PCs with different levels of security to tempt hackers. When these " honeypots " are hacked, the researchers are able to gather information about hacking and are then able to apply that knowledge to the development of better security systems.

Some hackers who penetrate secure websites subscribe to the belief that all information should be free and accessible. Others see themselves as taking an important role in protecting websites and feel that by gaining access to a site; they are identifying vulnerabilities in the security program. Still others, motivated by boredom and seeking entertainment, engage in recreational hacking and leave the sites they visit unchanged.

Can trespassing onto someone's website be considered parallel to trespassing into someone's physical property? Opponents of this are quick to point out the unclear boundaries and the ambiguity of ownership in cyberspace. As hacking becomes more prominent, society finds itself questioning the fine line between the free access to information and the rights of individual or corporate privacy.

Application writing

科技论文中如何引用参考文献
How to cite references of scientific papers

在科技论文之后列出参考文献是为了反映作者严谨的科学态度和所做研究工作的依据，也是维护知识产权的需要，参考文献是论文写作的一部分。

凡是引用其他作者的文章、观点、研究成果都应注明。可以引用的来源包括期刊、毕业论文、专著、专利等，公开发表的和未出版发表的都可以引用，未出版发表的要注明"In press"或者"forthcoming"。参考文献的引用要在原文引用处标明序号，在正文结束后有 Reference 一节，按照顺序列出各条文献条目。

1. 参考文献著录格式

（1）首字母顺序排列。将引用参考文献的作者姓氏放在参考条目的首位，并按照字母顺序编号排列。若一个作者有两篇文献被引用，则按照文献名称的第一个字母排列。

（2）出现的顺序排列。参考条目的格式一般遵循：著者，题（篇）名，刊名（书名），页次。

（3）著者部分。如果有多于3个作者，推荐使用第一个作者的姓名，后面加上"et al"。著者间加"，"，最后两著者间可以用"and"连接，也可以不用，但在一篇论文的参考文献中，风格要保持一致。

（4）刊名（书名）部分不要用斜体，如果是期刊，需要注明卷号、期号；如果是书名，需要注明出版年份。

（5）页次部分，注明引用内容的首页和末页。

2. 参考文献示例

References

[1] T. W. Barrett. History of ultrawideband(UWB) radar & communications: pioneers and innovators//Progress in Electromagnetics Symposium (PIERS'00). Cambridge, Mass: July 2000.

[2] B. Noel. Ed. Ultra-Wideband Radar: Proceedings of the First Los Alamos Symposium. Boca Raton, Fla: CRC Press, 1991.

[3] H. Bertoni, L. Carin, and L. Felsen. Eds. Ultra-Wideband Short-Pulse Electromagnetics. New York, NY: Plenum Press, 1993.

[4] C. E. Shannon. Communication in the presence of noise. Proceedings of the IRE, Vol. 37, No. 1, pp. 10 - 21, 1949.

[5] R. A. Scholtz, R. Weaver, E. Homier, et al. UWB radio deployment challenges // Proc. IEEE International Symposium on Personal, Indoor and Mobile Radio Communications (PIMRC '02), Vol. 1, pp. 620 - 625, September 2000.

[6] C. K. Rushforth. Transmitted-reference techniques for random or unknown channels. IEEE Trans. Inform. Theory, Vol. 10, No. 1, pp. 39 - 42, 1964.

[7] J. Foerster. Channel modeling sub-committee report final. IEEE P802. 15-02 /368r5-SG3a, December 2002, http: // ieee802. org/15/.

注：参考文献中人名后的"Eds."、"Ed."表示该书的"编者"。

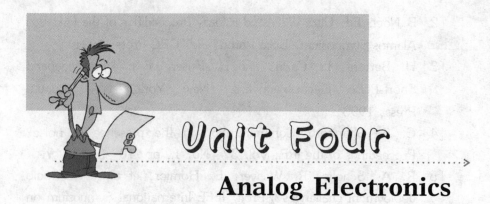

Unit Four
Analog Electronics

Goals

After studying this unit, you should be able to
- understand the history of analog electronics.
- memorize the main contents of analog electronics.
- apply analog electronics technology.

 Texts

■ Passage A

Introduction to Analog Electronics

The real electronics which is called today was actually started after the discovery of the **transistor effect**.[1] In Bell Labs[2], Shockley, Brattain, Bardeen et al. recognize the **amplification effect** in **semiconductors** through a series of experiments and observation. Small changes of weak current will have a huge impact, which is the "zoom" effect. Transistor opened the road for the electronics and more importantly it opened the road for the computing world.[3] Computers of various types started hitting the market and the research works got a boost. [4]

Transistor is the fundamental building block of modern electronic devices, and is used in radio, telephone, computer and other electronic systems. It is often cited as being one of the greatest achievements in the 20th century, and some consider it one of the most important technological breakthroughs in human history. [5]

A transistor is made of a solid piece of a semiconductor material, with at least three terminals connected to an external circuit. There are two types of standard **bipolar** transistors, NPN and PNP, with different circuit symbols (Fig. 4-1). The letters refer to layers of semiconductor material used. The NPN bipolar transistor consists of an N-type **emitter** (E), a P-type base (B), and an N-type collector (C).

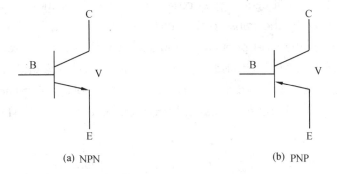

Fig. 4-1 Transistor circuit symbols

In electronics, a transistor is a semiconductor device commonly used to amplify or **switch** electronic signals.

The common emitter amplifier is designed so that a small change in voltage (V_{in}) changes the small base current and the collector current hugely changes, which means that small swings in V_{in} produce large changes in V_{out} (Fig. 4-2). Various configurations of single transistor amplifier are possible, with some providing current **gain**, some voltage gain, and some both.

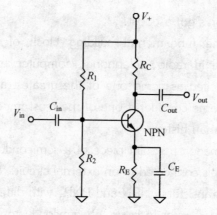

Fig. 4-2   CE (common emitter) amplifier

When a transistor is used as a switch, it must be either OFF or fully ON. In the fully ON state, the voltage V_{CE} is almost zero and the transistor is saturated, because it cannot pass collector current I_c any more. The output device switched by the transistor is usually called the "load".

Presently, the most popular technology for realizing microcircuits makes use of MOS transistors. It also has three polars, which are grid(G), drain (D) and source(S) respectively. According to the voltage condition, there are two kinds of MOS transistors: enhancement and exhausted. The symbols

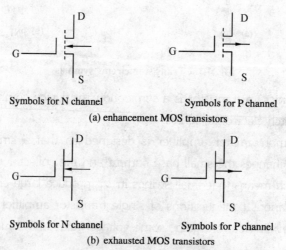

Fig. 4-3   MOS transistors

for enhancement MOS transistors and exhausted MOS transistors are shown in Fig. 4-3.

Based on transistors and MOS transistors, various circuits are manufactured which involve basic amplifier circuit, biasing circuit, multi-stage amplifier circuit, integrated operational amplifier circuit, power amplifier circuit, rectification circuit, regulation circuit, feedback amplifier, signal processing circuit, signal generator circuit, DC power supply, and so on.

■ Passage B

Integrated Circuits

Some other problems were also there like the assembling of the electronic components on a single mother board. Jack Kilby[6] in Texas Instruments found a very nice solution. He suggested throwing away all the wires and tried to connect the resistors, capacitors and transistors on the same piece of wafer internally. Surprisingly his ideas worked and gave birth to the integrated circuit industry.[7]

An integrated circuit (IC) is a small electronic device made out of semiconductor material. ICs (shown in Fig. 4-4) are used for a variety of devices, including microprocessors, audio and video equipment, and automobiles.[8]

Integrated circuits are usually called ICs or chips(Fig. 4-5). They are complex circuits, which have been etched onto tiny chips of semiconductor (silicon). The chip is packaged in a plastic holder with pins spaced on a 0.1 in. (2.54 mm) grid, which will fit the holes on stripboard and breadboard.[9] Very fine wires inside the package link the chip to the pins.

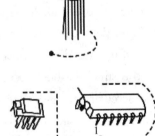

Fig. 4-4　Integrated circuits

The pins are numbered anti-clockwise around the IC (chip) starting near the notch or dot. They are easily damaged by heat when soldering and

Fig. 4-5　Examples of integrated circuits

their short pins cannot be protected with a heat sink. Instead we use a chip holder, strictly called a DIL(Digital Integrated Logic) socked, which can be safely soldered onto the circuit board. The chip is pushed into the holder when all soldering is completed. Chip holders are only needed when soldering so they are not used on breadboards.

Commercially produced circuit boards often have chips soldered directly to the board without a chip holder; usually this is done by a machine which is able to work very quickly.[10] Please don't attempt to do this yourself because you are likely to destroy the chip and it will be difficult to remove without damage by de-soldering.

If you need to remove a chip it can be gently prized out of the holder with a small flat-blade screwdriver. Carefully lever up each end by inserting the screwdriver blade between the chip and its holder and gently twist the screwdriver. Take care to start lifting at both ends before you attempt to remove the chip, otherwise you will bend and possibly break the pins.

Notes

[1] The real electronics which is called today was actually started after the discovery of the transistor effect.

今天所说的电子技术实际上是在发现晶体管效应以后开始（发

展)的。

[2] Bell Labs

贝尔实验室。贝尔实验室是晶体管、激光器、太阳能电池、发光二极管、数字交换机、通信卫星、电子数字计算机、蜂窝移动通信设备、长途电视传送、仿真语言、有声电影、立体声录音、通信网等许多重大发明的诞生地。自 1925 年以来，贝尔实验室共获得 2.5 万多项专利，现在，平均每个工作日获得 3 项多专利。贝尔实验室的使命是为客户创造、生产和提供富有创新性的技术，这些技术使朗讯科技(Lucent Technologies)公司在通信系统、产品、元件和网络软件方面处于全球领先地位。

[3] Transistor opened the road for the electronics and more importantly it opened the road for the computing world.

晶体管为电子技术开辟了道路，更重要的是，它为计算机世界开辟了道路。

[4] Computers of various types started hitting the market and the research works got a boost.

各种类型的计算机开始在市场上出现，研究工作进入一个迅速发展的时代。

[5] It (transistor) is often cited as being one of the greatest achievements in the 20th century, and some consider it one of the most important technological breakthroughs in human history.

晶体管被认为是 20 世纪最伟大的成就之一，有时也被认为是人类历史上最重要的技术突破之一。

[6] Jack Kilby

Jack Kilby 在 1958 年 9 月 12 日发明了微芯片，这个装置揭开了人类 20 世纪电子革命的序幕，同时宣告了数字时代的来临。微芯片是采用微电子技术制成的集成电路芯片，它已发展进入千兆(芯片 GSI)时代。

[7] He suggested throwing away all the wires and tried to connect the resistors,

capacitors and transistors on the same piece of wafer internally. Surprisingly his ideas worked and gave birth to the integrated circuit industry.

他提议不用任何导线,把电阻、电容和晶体管在同一片晶片内部连接起来,令人不可思议的是他的想法成功了,从此诞生了集成电路工业。

[8] ICs (shown in Fig. 4-4) are used for a variety of devices, including microprocessors, audio and video equipment, and automobiles.

在各种设备包括微处理器、音频和视频设备及汽车中都要用到集成电路(见图4-4)。

[9] The chip is packaged in a plastic holder with pins spaced on a 0.1 in. (2.54 mm) grid, which will fit the holes on stripboard and breadboard.

芯片封装在一个塑料插座上,引脚间距为0.1英寸(2.54毫米),这个距离与面包板和条形焊接板上的小孔距离相适应。

[10] Commercially produced circuit boards often have chips soldered directly to the board without a chip holder; usually this is done by a machine which is able to work very quickly.

在商业制作中,往往将芯片直接焊接在芯片插座上,并且通常由机器来完成,所以速度非常快。

Key words and phrases

analog electronics	模拟电子技术
transistor	晶体管
amplification	放大
semiconductor	半导体
current	电流
bipolar	双极型
emitter (E)	(晶体管的)发射极
base (B)	(晶体管的)基极

collector (C)	(晶体管的)集电极
switch	开关
voltage	电压
gain	增益
saturated	饱和的
load	负载
grid (G)	(MOS管的)栅极
drain (D)	(MOS管的)漏极
source (S)	(MOS管的)源极
enhancement MOS transistor	增强型金属氧化物半导体(MOS)管
exhausted MOS transistor	耗尽型金属氧化物半导体(MOS)管
bias circuit	偏置电路
operational amplifier circuit	运算放大电路
rectification	整流
regulation	稳压
DC power supply	直流电源
mother board	主板,母板
resistor	电阻
capacitor	电容
wafer	晶片
integrated circuit (IC)	集成电路
package	封装
pin	引脚
stripboard	条形焊接板
breadboard	面包板
anti-clockwise	逆时针方向
notch	凹槽

solder	焊接
heat sink	散热片
chip holder	芯片插座
screwdriver	螺丝起子

Exercises

1. Oral practice.

(1) Explain the unilateral conduction (单向导电性) of diode.

(2) What is the difference between "bipolar transistors" and "unipolar transistors"?

(3) Enumerate the analytical procedure of basic amplifier circuits.

(4) Describe the advantages of transistor amplifier circuits and MOS transistor amplifier circuits.

*(5) Which type of OPAMP have you used in application?

2. Fill in the blanks with the words or phrases given in the list below. Change the word form where necessary.

PNP	NPN	switch	regulation
chip holder	give birth to	transistor	make use of
IC	emitter	solder	amplify
chip	load	anti-clockwise	

(1) Integrated circuits are usually called _____ or _____.

(2) There are two types of standard bipolar transistors, _____ and _____. It consists of an _____, a base, and a

collector.

(3) The pins are numbered _____ around the IC starting near the notch or dot.

(4) Presently, the most popular technology for realizing microcircuits _____ MOS transistors.

(5) Jack Kilby suggested throwing away all the wires and tried to connect the resistors, capacitors and _____ on the same piece of wafer internally, which worked and _____ the integrated circuit industries.

(6) Chips are often _____ directly to the board without a _____ when we produce circuit boards by ourselves.

(7) The major functions of transistor are _____ and _____.

(8) _____ circuit keeps the output voltage constant during the electric network voltage (电网电压) or _____ changes.

3. Translate the following sentences into Chinese or English.

(1) According to the voltage condition, there are two kinds of MOS transistors: enhancement and exhausted.

(2) Based on transistors, various circuits are manufactured which involve practical amplifier circuit, biasing circuit, operational amplifiers circuit, and other circuits like rectification and regulation, and DC power supplies.

(3) 今天,我们更多地用金属氧化物半导体(MOS)晶体管来做集成电路。

(4) 一般的集成电路芯片的引脚个数有14脚、20脚、28脚,甚至更多。它们大多以逆时针方向排列。

4. Translate the following professional document.

Because the limitations of manufacturing technology, it is difficult to manufacture large capacitor and inductance in integrated circuits.

Therefore, direct coupled amplifier circuits are adopted. Direct coupling refers to a direct connection between the coupling circuit before and after stage. It has good frequency characteristics, and is able to amplify slowly changing signals. However, when the temperature changes or circuit parameters are slightly changed, the quiescent operating point（静态工作点）will be changed. The output voltage goes up and down deviated from the static value, which is called zero drift. It is also called temperature drift. To solve this problem, a differential amplifier is applied as the input stage of the multi-stage amplifier. It is good at suppress zero drift.

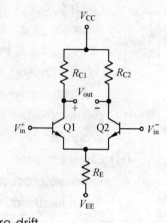

A differential amplifier is a type of electronic amplifier that amplifies the difference between two voltages but does not amplify the particular voltages.

Differential amplifiers are usually implemented with a basic circuit called long-tailed pair. This circuit was originally implemented using a pair of vacuum tubes. The circuit works the same way for all three-terminal devices with current gain. The long-tail resistor circuit bias points are largely determined by Ohm's Law and less so by active component characteristics.

5. Writing.

Please introduce the background of your major.

6. Introduction to National Undergraduate Electronic Design Contest（全国大学生电子设计竞赛）.

National Undergraduate Electronic Design Contest is one of the college students' academic competitions initiated by the Ministry of Education. It is a science and technology activity for the masses of students, and promotes the reform of information and electronics discipline curriculum and course contents, which aims at higher education reform. It is characterized by the contents related to the reform closely, in order to promote the teaching reform and laboratory construction. It has both theoretical design and practical manufacture, to fully test and strengthen the student's ability of basic theory and practice innovation.

National Undergraduate Electronic Design Contest holds in September of every odd year, lasting for four days. In the non-competition year, the regional competition(区赛)is organized.

Electronic circuit application (including analog and digital circuit design) is the main content, involving application of analog-digital hybrid circuit, SCM (单片机), programmable devices, EDA software and PC. Topics include "theory design" and "practical manufacture and debugging".

Topics can be divided into seven categories:

(1) power supply;

(2) signal source;

(3) high frequency radio;

(4) amplifier;

(5) instrumentation;

(6) data acquisition and processing;

(7) control.

During the competition, students can access the relevant paper or network information technology, discuss collective design ideas and determine the design scheme, to complete tasks as a team.

Then, acceptation (验收) is followed, i.e. a live demonstration. Sometimes, students may carry some necessary testing tools and accessories to carry on debugging (half an hour limited).

In the process of response (答辩), work principles and design thoughts are focused. For example, to achieve some functions, what is your design idea? How many options are there? Why do you choose this plan? What's its working principle? Which devices do you choose? Why? Does it matter without it?

Extended reading

Passage C

OPAMP (Operational Amplifier)

Many of the "processes" of signal processing are based on the use of an operational amplifier, especially at frequencies below a few megahertz. These processes include addition (summing) of two or more signals, multiplication, integration, precise rectification and active filtering.

OPAMP internal is actually a high-gain direct-coupled amplifier. Its internal block diagram is shown in Fig. 4-6. It is composed of four parts: input stage, middle stage, output stage and bias circuit.

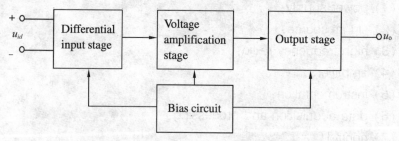

Fig. 4-6 Internal block diagram of OPAMP

1. Input stage

Input stage is a key part to improve the quality of operational amplifier. It has high input-impedance. In order to reduce zero drift and suppress interference jamming of common-mode signal, input stage apply differential amplifier circuit with a constant current source, which is also called differential input stage.

2. Middle stage

The main role of middle stage is to provide a large enough voltage magnification, so it is also known as voltage amplification stage. It is required that the middle stage itself has a high voltage gain.

3. Output stage

The main role of output stage is to output sufficient current to meet the needs of the load. At the same time, it is required to have low output resistance and high input resistance, in order to isolate amplification stage and load.

4. Bias circuit

The main role of bias circuit is to provide appropriate working current of all stages. Generally, it is composed of different constant current sources.

The amplifier has two inputs, and it is called a differential amplifier because its output is proportional to the difference between the two input voltages V_+ and V_- (shown in Fig. 4-7).

$$V_o = A(V_+ - V_-)$$

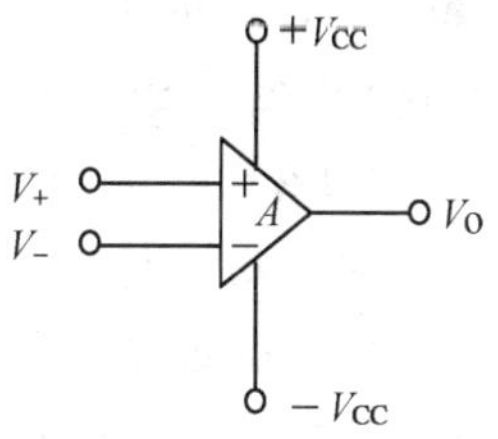

The input impedance is quite high;

Fig. 4-7 Operational amplifiers

typically a resistance of a few megohms shunted by a tiny capacitance.

Operational amplifiers used as amplifiers (they have other uses, too) are usually operated in negative feedback circuits, which set the gain, bandwidth and other features as the required well-defined values. The simplest example is the voltage follower.

■ Passage D

Power Supplies

Most electronic circuits obtain their operating power from DC voltage supplies. Some circuits, especially in portable equipments such as radios, mobile phones and laptop computers which consume low power, use batteries to provide the DC voltages directly. Other equipments use electronic power supplies to provide the required DC voltages. These power supplies obtain their power from the AC electricity supply of 230 V at 50 Hz in Europe, or 115 V at 60 Hz in America.

There are three main types, as shown in Fig. 4-8.

- The simple unregulated linear supply, shown in Fig. 4-8(a). This uses a transformer to convert the AC input to a lower voltage, usually in the range 6 – 24 V, followed by a rectifier to convert the low-voltage AC to DC, and a capacitor which filters out most of the supply frequency "ripple", leaving a fairly smooth DC output voltage.

- The regulated linear supply, shown in Fig. 4-8(b). This is basically an unregulated supply followed by an electronic regulator circuit to "regulate" the output. The regulator uses analog circuit techniques to hold the output voltage constant in spite of changes in the AC supply voltage or in the output load current.

- The switched-mode supply, shown in Fig. 4-8(c). This type is widely used in television receivers and personal computers, and other equipments which uses a number of different voltage supplies. Its

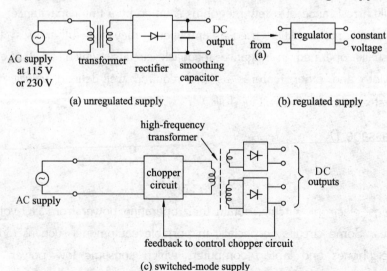

Fig. 4-8　The DC power supplies

main advantage, in such equipment, is that the bulky and heavy supply frequency input transformer of the linear supply is replaced by much smaller, lighter and cheaper components.

The input AC supply is rectified directly to DC, and this high-voltage DC is "chopped" into AC at a rate just above the highest audible frequency, typically about 40 kHz. (Otherwise the chopping would be heard as a whistle.) This AC voltage is converted to several different voltages by a transformer which, because it works at a much higher frequency, is much smaller and lighter than the linear-supply equivalent. (It also provides the electrical isolation needed for safety.) The transformer outputs are rectified and smoothed to provide the low-voltage d. c. supplies and, in computer monitors and TV sets using CRT(Cothade Ray Tube)displays, an "extra-high-tension" (EHT) supply, typically at 25 kV. Regulation can be achieved by sensing one of the output voltages and feeding-back a correction signal to the chopper circuit to adjust the power fed from the input supply to the transformer.

 Application writing

感谢信

Letter of thanks

感谢信是集体单位或个人对关心、帮助、支持本单位或个人表示衷心感谢的函件。在日常生活和工作中,得到人家的帮助和支持,可用这种文体"感谢"一下。它与表扬信有许多相似之处,所不同的是感谢信也有表扬信的意思,但是重点在感谢。

1. 感谢信的格式

感谢信的格式一般由标题、称谓、正文、结语,以及署名与日期5个部分组成。

(1) 标题。可只写"感谢信"三字,也可加上感谢对象或事由。

(2) 称谓。写感谢对象的单位名称或个人姓名。

(3) 正文。主要写两层意思,一是写感谢对方的理由,即"为什么感谢";二是直接表达感谢之意。

(4) 结语。一般用"此致敬礼"或"再次表示诚挚的感谢"之类的话,也可自然结束正文,不写结语。

(5) 署名与日期。

注意:写感谢信时文字要简洁,篇幅不宜太长;措辞要自然,诚恳亲切。

2. 感谢信的示例

Thank You for Interview

Dear Mr. Zhang,

  I appreciate your meeting with me yesterday to discuss the electronic engineer position. I was very impressed by both your enthusasm and the excellent work in your organization.

  If you have any further questions, you may write to my address or call me at (010) ×××××××.

Sincerely yours,
Wang Jun

Unit Five
Digital Logic Circuits

Goals

After studying the unit, you should be able to
- define the digital signal and the digital system.
- memorize the main contents of digital logic circuits.
- apply HDLs to the design of digital logic circuits.

 *Texts*

■ Passage A

Digital Logic Circuits

    Digital logic circuits study the digital signal. So first of all, two concepts must be distinguished, which are the pulse signal and the digital signal. In narrow sense, the pulse signal is a signal that suddenly effects in a short time. In broad sense, any kind of signal can be called a pulse signal, except sine wave or signal composed with several sine waves.[1] The pulse signal is not continuous, but is generally periodic.

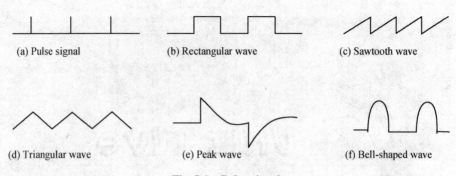

Fig. 5-1 Pulse signals

A digital signal is a two-level rectangular wave, usually with "1" indicating the high level, "0" the low level. Periodically dividing the rectangular wave, we can get a combination of symbols of 0 and 1, i.e. "110100011". A digital signal is also one kind of pulse signals.

Digital electronics is a "logical" science. Logic, generally speaking, is the science of formal principles of reasoning. Digital logic is the science of reasoning with numbers. The number system with which we are most familiar is the base 10, or decimal system. Recent technological developments have created the need for other number systems, such as the binary (base 2), octal (base 8), and hexadecimal (base 16).[2]

In an algebra proposed by George Boole about 1850, the variables are permitted to have only two values—true or false, usually written as 1 and 0, and the algebraic operations on the variables are limited to those defined as AND, OR, NOT.[3]

A special circuit called a gate can perform nearly all-digital functions. The basic gates are AND gate, OR gate and NOT gate (shown in Fig. 5-2). If the logic operation is too complex for one gate, it can almost always be implemented through the use of a combination of gates.[4] These extended logic circuits are called combinational logic circuits. In combinational logic circuits, the output, at any time, only depends on the present input, having nothing to do with the original status.

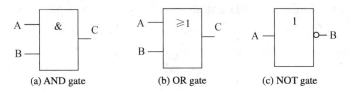

(a) AND gate (b) OR gate (c) NOT gate

Fig. 5-2 Symbols of gate

The typical devices of combinational logic circuits are encoder, decoder, data selector, numeric comparator, and parity checker. To analyze them, there are three steps. First, an output expression is written. Then, a truth table is drawn according to the expression. At last, the logic function is got.

Flip-flops are important components of sequential logic circuits. Typical flip-flops include basic RS-FF, clocked RS-FF (shown in Fig. 5-3), clocked D-FF, clocked JK-FF, and clocked T-FF.[5]

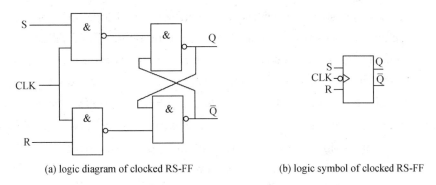

(a) logic diagram of clocked RS-FF (b) logic symbol of clocked RS-FF

Fig. 5-3 Clocked RS-FF

Compared with a combinational logic circuit, the output of a sequential logic circuit depends on not only the present input, but also the original status. Register and counter are typical devices of a sequential logic circuit. To analyze this circuit, three steps are followed. Firstly, equations are written, which include output equation, driving equation and state equation. Then the state transition table, state transition diagram or sequential chart is drawn. Finally the logic function is got.

There are also digital integrated circuits, which have 74 series (civil) and 54 series (**military**). There are several families of logic chips numbered from 74××00 onwards with letters (××) in the middle of the number to indicate the type of circuitry, e.g. 74LS00 and 74HC00.

The 74LS (Low-power Schottky) family uses TTL (Transistor-Transistor Logic) circuitry, which is fast but requires more power than later families.

The 74HC family has high-speed CMOS circuitry. They are CMOS chips with the same pin arrangements as the older 74LS family. Note that 74HC inputs cannot be reliably driven by 74LS outputs because the voltage ranges used for logic 0 are not quite compatible.[6]

■ **Passage B**

Register and Counter

Register and shift register are common sequential logic circuits. They are logic components used to temporarily store numbers. Their difference is that the shift register has a shift function that register doesn't have.

A register is a group of flip-flops with each flip-flop capable of storing one bit of information. Besides the flip-flops, a register may have combinational gates that perform certain data-processing tasks. The flip-flops hold the binary information and the gates control when new information is transferred into the register.

Various registers are available commercially. The simplest register is one that consists of only flip-flops, with no external gates. Fig. 5-4 shows such a register constructed with four D-FFs. The common clock input **triggers** all flip-flops on the **positive edge** of each pulse, and the binary data available at the four inputs are transferred into the 4-bit register.[7] The four outputs can be sampled at any time to obtain the binary information stored in the register. The clear input goes to a special terminal in each flip-flop. When it goes to 0, all flip-flops are reset **asynchronously**. It must be maintained at logic 1 during normal clocked operation. Note that the clock signal enables the D input, but that the clear input is independent of the clock. [8]

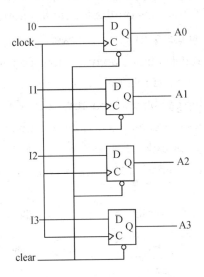

Fig. 5-4 4-bit register

The transfer of new information into a register is referred to as loading the register. If all the bits of the register are loaded simultaneously with a common clock pulse transition, we say that the loading is done in parallel. A clock transition applied to the register of Fig. 5-4 will load all four inputs I0 through I3 in parallel.

In digital system, counters are also widely used, which have functions such as timing, counting, **frequency division**, generating clock pulse and sequence pulse, and so on, because it can count the number of pulses.

There are numerous types of counters. According to the connection of flip-flops clock in counters, they can be divided into synchronous counters and asynchronous counters. Based on the way of counting, they can be divided into binary counters, decimal counters, and counters of **arbitrary numerical system**. In accordance with the state changing laws, counters are divided into adding counters, subtracting counters and adding /subtracting counters. [9]

In synchronous counters, under the control of the parallel clock pulse, the states of flip-flops change at the same time. In contrast, system clock of asynchronous counters only acts on the lowest flip-flop, and clock of higher flip-flop is controlled by the output of the lower flip-flop.[10] Since each flip-flop has a transmission delay time, asynchronous counter works slower than synchronous counter, but has relatively simple circuit structure.

CT74161 is a typical binary counter, and CT74160 is a decimal counter. Based on these counters, counters of arbitrary numerical system can be formed through **cascade**. For example, two sexagesimal(六十进制的) counters and a duodecimal(十二进制的) counter are needed in order to make a digital clock.

Adding counters and subtracting counters are illustrated in Fig. 5-5.

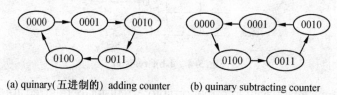

(a) quinary(五进制的) adding counter   (b) quinary subtracting counter

Fig. 5-5 Adding counters and substracting counters

Notes

[1] In broad sense, any kind of signal can be called a pulse signal, except a sine wave or signal composed with several sine waves.

　　从广义上来讲，任何一种信号都可以被称为脉冲信号，除了正弦波或由多个正弦波合成的信号。

[2] Recent technological developments have created the need for other number systems, such as the binary (base 2), octal (base 8), and hexadecimal (base 16).

　　近年来，科技的发展需要产生其他的数字系统，如二进制(基为2)、八进制(基为8)和十六进制(基为16)。

[3] In an algebra proposed by George Boole about 1850, the variables are permitted to have only two values—true or false, usually written

as 1 and 0, and the algebraic operations on the variables are limited to those defined as AND, OR, NOT.

乔治·布尔(英国数学家和逻辑学家)大约在 1850 年提出的代数学中,变量值只有两种:真和假,通常记为 1 和 0,代数运算也仅局限于与、或、非。

[4] If the logic operation is too complex for one gate, it can almost always be implemented through the use of a combination of gates.

如果逻辑运算太复杂,无法用一个门来实现,也可以通过几个门的组合来实现这个逻辑运算。

[5] Typical flip-flops include basic RS-FF, clocked RS-FF (shown in Fig. 5-2), clocked D-FF, clocked JK-FF, and clocked T-FF.

典型的触发器有基本 RS 触发器、钟控 RS 触发器(见图 5-2)、钟控 D 触发器、钟控 JK 触发器和钟控 T 触发器。

[6] Note that 74HC inputs cannot be reliably driven by 74LS outputs because the voltage ranges used for logic 0 are not quite compatible.

请注意,74LS 的输出不能可靠地驱动 74HC,因为两者用于逻辑 0 的电压范围不兼容。

[7] The common clock input triggers all flip-flops on the positive edge of each pulse, and the binary data available at the four inputs are transferred into the 4-bit register.

所有的触发器在同一时钟输入脉冲的上升沿触发,这时在 4 个输入端的二进制数据信息被传送到 4 位寄存器中。

[8] It must be maintained at logic 1 during normal clocked operation. Note that the clock signal enables the D input, but that the clear input is independent of the clock.

清零输入(在时钟正常控制工作时)必须保持为逻辑 1,注意时钟信号可以控制 D 的输入,但清零输入却与时钟无关(不受时钟信号控制的)。

[9] According to the connection of flip-flops clock in counters, they can be divided into synchronous counters and asynchronous counters. Based on the way of counting, they can be divided into binary

counters, decimal counters, and counters of arbitrary numerical system. In accordance with the state changing laws, counters are divided into adding counters, subtracting counters and adding / subtracting counters.

根据计数器中触发器时钟端的连接方式,可以分为同步和异步计数器。基于计数方式,可分为二进制计数器、十进制计数器和任意进制的计数器。根据状态变化规律,又可分为加法计数器、减法计数器和加/减法计数器。

[10] In contrast, system clock of asynchronous counters only acts on the lowest flip-flop, and clock of the higher flip-flop is controlled by the output of the lower flip-flop.

相反,异步计数器的系统时钟只作用于最低一位触发器,高位触发器的时钟由低位触发器的输出控制。

Key words and phrases

digital logic circuit	数字逻辑电路
high level	高电平
low level	低电平
rectangular wave	方波
digital electronics	数字电子技术
decimal	十进制
binary	二进制
octal	八进制
hexadecimal	十六进制
algebra	代数学
variable	变量
gate	门电路
combinational logic circuit	组合逻辑电路
encoder	编码器
decoder	译码器

data selector	数据选择器
numeric comparator	数值比较器
parity checker	奇偶校验器
output expression	输出方程
truth table	真值表
flip-flop	触发器
sequential logic circuit	时序逻辑电路
register	寄存器
counter	计数器
driving equation	驱动方程
state equation	状态方程
sequential chart	时序图
civil	民用的
military	军用的
D-FF	D触发器
trigger	触发
positive edge	上升沿
asynchronously	异步地
simultaneously	同步地
frequency division	分频
arbitrary	任意的
cascade	级联,〈微软〉层叠,阶梯式显示法

Exercises

1. Oral practice.

(1) How do you transform a decimal number to a binary number?

(2) Introduce the background of digital logic circuits.
(3) What are the modern methods of digital system designing?
(4) How do you design a digital clock with Verilog HDL?

2. Fill in the blanks with the words or phrases given in the list below. Change the word form where necessary.

decoder	clear	sequential logic circuit
depend on	sequential chart	flip-flop
simultaneous	truth table	have nothing to do with
clock pulse	data processing	gate
cascade	positive edge	

(1) In a combinational logic circuit, the output, at any time, only _____ the present input, _____ the original status.

(2) An n-bit register has a group of n _____ and is capable of storing any joinery information of n bits, and it also has _____ that perform certain _____ tasks.

(3) If all the bits of the register are loaded _____ with a common clock pulse transition, we say that the loading is done in parallel.

(4) _____ can translate the binary code standing for formation into corresponding high or low output level.

(5) _____ is the method to extend the function based on existing logic chips.

(6) According to the _____ of combinational logic circuit, the logic function is got, and the function of _____ is got from state transition diagram.

(7) Generally, a counter has inputs named CP and CR, which stands for _____ and _____.

(8) In sequential logic circuits, some are triggered by high/low level, others are _____ or negative edge.

3. Translate the following sentences into English.

(1) 所有的组合逻辑电路都可以由与、或、非三种基本门电路来组成。

(2) 触发器是时序逻辑电路的一个重要组成部分。

(3) 一个 n 位寄存器一般由 n 个触发器及若干组合门电路构成，可以储存 n 位的二进制信息，并完成一定的数据处理任务。

(4) 如果是同步清零，清零端必须结合时钟信号才能实现清零功能；而如果是异步清零，清零端与时钟信号无关。

4. Translate the following professional document.

An ADC is a device that converts a continuous physical quantity (usually voltage) to a digital number that represents the quantity's amplitude. The conversion involves quantization of the input, so it necessarily introduces a small amount of error. Instead of doing a single conversion, an ADC often performs the conversions periodically. The result is a sequence of digital values that have converted a continuous-time and continuous-amplitude analog signal to a discrete-time and discrete-amplitude digital signal.

An ADC is defined by its bandwidth (the range of frequencies it can measure) and its signal to noise ratio (how accurately it can measure a signal relative to the noise it introduces). The actual bandwidth of an ADC is characterized primarily by its sampling rate, and to a lesser extent by how it handles errors such as aliasing (混叠). The dynamic range of an ADC is influenced by many factors, including the resolution (the number of output levels it can quantize a signal to), linearity and accuracy (how well the quantization levels match the true analog signal) and jitter (small timing errors that introduce additional noise).

The inverse operation is performed by a digital-to-analog converter (DAC).

5. Writing.

Suppose that you will graduate this year, write your resume.

6. Simulate English interviews in groups.

求职英语面试常见对话

Q: Can you sell yourself in two minutes? Go for it.

A: With my qualifications and experience, I feel I am hardworking, responsible and diligent in any project I undertake. Your organization could benefit from my analytical and interpersonal skills.

Q: What are your strongest traits?

A: Helpfulness and caring. /Adaptability and a sense of humor. / Cheerfulness and friendliness.

Q: How do you rate yourself as a professional?

A: With my strong academic background, I am capable and competent.

Q: What do you think you are worth to us?

A: I feel I can make some positive contributions to your company in the future.

Q: What makes you think you would be a success in this position?

A: My graduate school training combined with my internship should qualify me for this particular job. I am sure I will be successful.

Q: How do you handle your conflict with your colleagues in your work?

A: I will try to present my ideas in a more clear and civilized manner in order to get my points across.

Extended reading

Passage C

Hardware Description Languages

This text introduces you to the overall concept of hardware description languages and explains their many advantages over other methods of design entry, particularly schematic capture, for designing large, complex systems.

Years ago, as integrated circuits grew in complexity, a better method for designing them was needed. Schematic capture tools had been developed which allowed an engineer to draw schematics on a computer screen to represent a circuit. This worked well because graphic representations are always useful to understand small but complex functions. But as chip density increased, schematic capture of these circuits became unwieldy and difficult to use for the design of large circuits. The transistor densities of application specific integrated circuits(ASICs) and Field Programmable Gate Arrays(FPGAs) grew to the point where a better tool was needed. That tool is a Hardware Description Language(HDL). As more engineers design complex systems on a chip, they have no option but to use HDLs. The major advantages of HDLs are:

- Ability to handle large, complex designs
- Different levels of abstraction
- Top-down design
- Reusability
- Concurrency
- Timing
- Optimization
- Standards
- Documentation

Hardware description languages use statements, like programming language statements, in order to define, simulate, synthesize, and layout hardware. The two main HDLs are verilog and VHDL[VHSIC(Very High Speed Integrated Circuit) Hardware Description Language]. There are other, limited capability, languages such as ABEL, CUPL, and PALASM that are tailored specifically for designing PLAs(Programmable Logic Arrays) and CPLDs(Complex Programmable Logic Devices). They are not robust enough to cover the complexity required for most FPGAs and ASICs. However, both verilog and VHDL can be used to design anything from the most complex ASIC to the least complex PAL (Programmable Array Logic).

A hardware description language can be used to design at any level of abstraction from high-level architectural models to low-level switch models. These levels, from least amount of detail to most amount of detail, are given in Table 5-1. The top two levels use what are called behavioral models, while the lower three levels use what are called structural models.

Table 5-1 Different levels of abstraction

Algorithmic level	Behavioral models
Architectural level	
Register transfer level(RTL)	Structural models
Gate level	
Switch level	

■ Passage D

PLD(Programmable Logic Device)

The first piece of PLD(Programmable Logic Device) is PROM (Programmable Read-only Memory), which was occurred in 1970, followed by PLA, PAL, GAL (Gemeric Array Logic), EPLD (Erasable Programmable Logic Device) and the CPLD, FPGA, and so on. The emergence of PLD not only changes the traditional design method of digital systems, but also promotes the rapid development of EDA (Electronic Design Automation) technology. EDA is a tool to replace the person to complete a variety of complex logic synthesis, placement, simulation and design during designing digital systems, which is based on computer technology. Designers use hardware description language to describe system functions, which can be completed by computer software on its own, and gain the design results. EDA tools improve the design efficiency greatly.

1. Classification by integration density

PLD can be divided into two classifications according to the integration density: LDPLD (Low-density Programmable Logic Device) and HDPLD (High-density Programmable Logic Device).

LDPLD usually refers to PLD which was early developed and whose integration density is less than 700, such as ROM, PLA, PAL, GAL, and so on.

HDPLD includes EPLD, CPLD (Complex PLD) and FPGA. And its integration density is greater than 700. Such as Altera's EPM9560, whose density is 12,000, Lattice's ispLSI3320 (In-system Programmable Large Scale Integration 3320) is 14,000. At present, the most highly integrated HDPLD is up to 250,000.

2. Classification by programming mode

There are two programming modes of PLD: OTP (One Time Programmable) and MTP (Many Time Programmable).

OTP devices are single-use devices, only allowing users to program once, which can not be changed after programming. The advantages are high reliability and high integration, strong anti-interference.

MTP devices are reused devices, allowing users to program, to modify or to design several times. It is particularly suited to the development of prototype system and junior designers.

According to the structure and programming mode of PLD, it can be divided into four categories:

(1) programmable devices using one-time programmable fuse or anti-fuse, such as PROM, PAL and EPLD (Erasable Programmable Logic Device).

(2) programmable devices using ultraviolet erase, power programmable components, namely multiple programmable devices using EPROM (Erasable and Programmable Read-only Memory), UVCMOS structure.

(3) programmable devices using electrical erase, power programmable components. One of those is E^2PROM, and the other is multiple programming device using flash memory modules.

(4) multiple programming devices based on SRAM (Static Random Access Memory) structure. At present, the majority of FPGA are based on SRAM structure.

3. Classification by structural characteristics

According to the structural characteristics, PLD can be divided into two classifications: array-based PLD and field programmable gate array-based FPGA.

Array-based PLD are basically composed of AND arrays and OR arrays. Simple PLD (such as PROM, PLA, PAL and GAL), EPLD and CPLD are array-based PLD.

Field programmable gate array-based FPGA has structures of gate array. Many programmable units (or logic function blocks) are field programmable gate array-based FPGA, known as cell type PLD.

 Application writing

简历
Resume

简历,顾名思义,就是对个人学历、经历、特长、爱好及其他有关情况所进行的简明扼要的书面介绍。

1. 简历的内容

英文简历的内容和中文简历没有什么很大的区别，一般应包括以下几个方面的内容。

（1）个人资料：姓名、性别、出生年月、家庭地址、政治面貌、婚姻状况、身体状况等；

（2）学业相关内容：就读学校、所学专业、学位、外语及计算机掌握程度等；

（3）本人经历：入学以来的简单经历，主要是担任社会工作或加入党团等方面的情况；

（4）所获荣誉；

（5）本人特长：如计算机、外语、文艺、体育等。

注意：在写英文简历时，简历中的英文不能出现任何语法错误或者拼写错误。因此，英文简历宜简不宜繁，篇幅不要太长。

2. 简历的格式

英文简历的格式和中文简历也大致相同，主要有以下几种。

（1）时序型格式

时序型格式以渐进的顺序罗列你曾就职的职位，从最近的职位开始，然后再回溯。你要说明你的责任、该职位所需要的技能及最关键的、突出的成就。关注的焦点在于时间、工作持续期、成长与进步及成就。

（2）功能型格式

功能型格式在简历的一开始就强调技能、能力、资信、资质及成就，但是并不把这些内容与某个特定雇主联系在一起。

（3）综合型格式

首先扼要地介绍你的市场价值（功能型格式），随即列出你的工作经历（时序型格式）。这种综合型格式很受欢迎。功能部分信息充实，有阅读者感兴趣的材料而且工作经历部分的内容又能够强有力地作为佐证加以支持。

3. 简历的示例

<u>Yan Zheng</u>

Room 212, Building 343

Tsinghua University, Beijing, 100084

Tel: 010-62771234

Personal Particulars

Sex: M

Date of Birth: 20 September, 1988

Age: 26

Place of Birth: Beijing

Email: good@tsinghua.edu.cn

Objective

Obtain a challenging position as a software engineer with an emphasis on software design and development.

Education

2011.9 - 2014.6 Dept. of Automation, Graduate School of Tsinghua University, M.E.

2007.9 - 2011.7 Dept. of Automation, Beijing Institute of Technology, B.E.

Academic Main Courses

Mathematics

Advanced Mathematics, Probability and Statistics, Linear Algebra, Engineering Mathematics, Numerical Algorithm, Operational Algorithm, Functional Analysis, Linear and Nonlinear Programming

Electronics and Computer

Circuit Principal, Data Structures, Digital Electronics, Artificial Intelligence, Computer, Local Area Network

Computer Abilities

Be skilled in use of MS FrontPage, Win 2000/XP, JavaBeans, HTML, CGI,

JavaScript, Perl, Visual Interdev, Distributed Objects, CORBA, C, C^{++}, Protel 99, Pascal, PL/I and SQL software

English Skills

Have a good command of both spoken and written English. Passed CET-6 TOEFL: 115; GRE: 2213

Scholarship and Awards

2013.3　　Guanghua First-class Scholarship for graduate

2012.11　 Metal Machining Practice Award

2011.4　　Academic Progress Award

Qualifications

Have general business knowledge related to financial and healthcare. Be passion for the Internet, and abundance of common sense.

A Useful Glossary for Personal Data
（个人资料常用词汇）

name	姓名
age	年龄
height	身高
weight	体重
birthplace	出生地点
birth date	出生日期（date of birth 出生日期）
nationality	民族,国籍（citizenship 国籍）
native place	籍贯
marital status	婚姻状况
family status	家庭状况
married	已婚
single	未婚
health condition	健康状况
short-sighted	近视
far-sighted	远视
home phone	住宅电话
work/office phone	办公电话
current address	目前住址

postal code	邮政编码
province	省
city	市
county	县
autonomous region	自治区
district	区
street	街
road	路
lane	胡同,巷
house number	门牌

A Useful Glossary for Educational Background(教育程度常用词汇)

educational history	学历
educational background	教育程度
curriculum	课程
major	主修
minor	副修
social practice	社会实践
part-time job	业余工作,兼职工作
summer job	暑期工作
vacation job	假期工作
extracurricular activity	课外活动
academic activity	学术活动
social activity	社会活动
rewards	奖励
scholarship	奖学金

excellent League member	优秀团员
excellent leader	优秀干部
student council	学生会
off-job training	脱产培训
in-job training	在职培训
educational system	学制
academic year	学年
semester	〈美〉学期
term	〈英〉学期
supervisor	论文导师
student teaching	教学实习
pass	及格
fail	不及格
marks	分数
examination	考试
degree	学位
post doctorate	博士后
doctor	博士
master	硕士
bachelor	学士
graduate student	研究生
abroad student	留学生
undergraduate	大学肄业生
government-supported student	公费生
commoner	自费生
intern	实习生
prize fellow	奖学金获得者

A Useful Glossary for Personal Character(个人品质常用词汇)

able	有才干的,能干的
adaptable	适应性强的
active	主动的,活跃的
aggressive	有进取心的
ambitious	有雄心壮志的
analytical	善于分析的
apprehensive	有理解力的
aspiring	有志气的,有抱负的
audacious	大胆的,有冒险精神的
capable	有能力的,有才能的
candid	正直的
competent	能胜任的
constructive	建设性的
cooperative	有合作精神的
creative	富创造力的
dedicated	有奉献精神的
dependable	可靠的
diplomatic	老练的,有策略的
disciplined	守纪律的
dutiful	尽职的
well-educated	受过良好教育的
efficient	有效率的
energetic	精力充沛的
expressivity	善于表达,表达性
faithful	守信的,忠诚的
frank	直率的,真诚的

generous	宽宏大量的
genteel	有教养的
gentle	有礼貌的
humorous	幽默的
impartial	公正的
independent	有主见的
industrious	勤奋的
ingenious	有独创性的
motivated	目的明确的
intelligent	理解力强的
logical	合乎逻辑的,有逻辑头脑的
methodical	有条理的,办事有条不紊的
modest	谦虚的
objective	客观的
precise	一丝不苟的
punctual	严守时刻的
realistic	实事求是的
responsible	负责的
sensible	明白事理的
sporting	光明正大的
systematic	有系统的
sweet-tempered	性情温和的
tireless	孜孜不倦的

Unit Six

An Important Communication Tool—MATLAB

Goals

After studying the unit, you should be able to
- describe what is MATLAB.
- explain the functions of MATLAB.
- explain the methods to draw a 2-D and 3-D figure.
- explain the differences between M files and C, C^{++} languages.

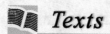 *Texts*

■ Passage A

MATLAB Summary

The name MATLAB stands for matrix laboratory. MATLAB was originally written to provide easy access to matrix software developed by the LINPACK and EISPACK projects.[1] Today, MATLAB uses software developed by the LAPACK and ARPACK projects, which together represent the state-of-the-art in software for matrix computation.

MATLAB has evolved over a period of years with input from many users. It is produced by MathWorks*, as shown in Fig. 6-1. In university environments, it is the standard instructional tool for introductory and advanced courses in mathematics, engineering, and science. In industry, MATLAB is the tool of choice for high-productivity research, development, and analysis.

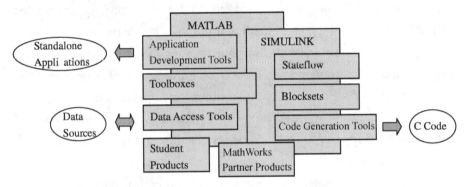

* The MathWorks offers a set of integrated products for data analysis, visualization, application development, simulation, design, and code generation. MATLAB is the foundation for all the MathWorks products.

Fig. 6-1 The MathWorks product family

MATLAB is an **intuitive** language and a technical computing environment. With a use community more than 500,000 strong spread throughout industry, government, and academia, MATLAB is the recognized standard worldwide for technical computing.[2] MATLAB is used in a variety of application areas, including signal and image processing, control system design, earth and life sciences, finance and economics, and instrumentation. The open architecture makes it easy to use MATLAB and companion products to explore data and create custom tools that provide early insights and competitive advantages. Simulink is a simulation and prototyping environment for modeling, simulating, and analyzing real world, dynamic systems. Simulink provides a block diagram interface that is built on the core MATLAB numeric, graphics, and programming functionality.

Passage B

Description Topics of MATLAB

1. Working in the flexible MATLAB environment

The MATLAB environment is designed for interactive or automated computation. Using the built-in math and graphics functions and easy-to-use tools, you can analyze and visualize your data on the fly.[3] The structured language and programming tools let you save the results of your interactive explorations and develop your own algorithms and applications.

Users working on a broad range of applications with various levels of complexity have found MATLAB to be an effective and flexible environment that grows with them.[4]

2. Trusted mathematics and numeric computing functions

With more than 600 mathematical, statistical, and engineering functions, MATLAB gives you immediate access to high-performance numeric computing. The numerical routines are fast, accurate, and reliable. These algorithms, developed by experts in mathematics, are the foundation of the MATLAB language. The core math engines incorporate the well-respected LAPACK and BLAS linear algebra subroutine libraries and FFTW signal processing library, which is a C subroutine library for computing the discrete Fourier transform(DFT) in one or more dimensions, of arbitrary input size, and of both real and complex data(as well as of even/odd data, i.e. the discrete cosine/sine transforms or DCT/DST), embedding the state-of-the-art in mathematical computation directly into MATLAB.

The math is optimized for matrix and vector operations, so you can use it in place of low-level languages like C and C^{++}, with equal performance but less programming. With an extensive collection of optimized math routines built right in, MATLAB frees engineers and scientists to focus on their real work, avoiding the time-consuming tasks of looking for, developing, debugging, and maintaining homegrown codes.[5]

MATLAB provides many functions for performing mathematical operations and analyzing data, including functions for working with:

(1) **Matrices** and linear algebra—matrix arithmetic, linear equations, singular values, and matrix factorizations.

(2) **Polynomials** and **interpolation**—standard polynomial operations such as polynomial roots, evaluation, differentiation, curve fitting and partial fraction expansion.

(3) **Signal processing**—digital filters, fast Fourier transforms(FFTs), and convolution.

(4) **Data analysis** and **statistics**—descriptive statistics, data pre-processing, regression, curve fitting, data filtering.

(5) **Function** functions—MATLAB functions that work with mathematical functions instead of numeric arrays, including plotting, optimization, zero finding, and numerical integration(quadrature).

(6) **Differential equations**—solving differential equation problems including: initial value problems for ordinary differential equations(ODEs) and differential algebraic equations(DAEs), delay differential equations, boundary value problems for ODEs, and initial-boundary value problems for systems of parabolic and elliptic partial differential equations(PDEs).

(7) **Sparse** matrices—covering both specialized and general mathematical operations, including iterative methods for sparse linear equations.

3. Revealing graphics provide insights into your data

MATLAB includes the specialized graphics in engineering and science. From 2-D line plots of raw data to labeled contour plots and interactive GUIs, these tools provide visual modeling capabilities to help you to understand complex systems. With MATLAB, you can customize virtually any aspect of your plots and produce high-equality graphics for written and live presentations.

MATLAB provides immediate access to specialized graphics features, including:

(1) 2-D and 3-D plot types such as line, log, histogram, function, mesh, surface, sphere, and patch objects;

(2) support for triangulated data and grid data;

(3) volume visualization for viewing scalar and vector data;

(4) image display and file I/O;

(5) interactive plot annotation and editing;

(6) OpenGL[6] rendering supported with hardware and software;

(7) quiver, ribbon, scatter, bar, pie, and stem plots;

(8) animation (movies) and sound;

(9) multiple light sources for colored surfaces;

(10) camera-based viewing and perspective control;

(11) interactive and programmatic control of individual plot attributes, such as line, axes, figure, legend, and paper;

(12) point-and-click GUI(Graphic User Interface)-building tools and programming API(Application Programming Interface);

(13) importing common graphical file formats, such as TIFF, JPEG, PNG, BMP, HDF, AVI, and PCX[7];

(14) printing and exporting graphics to other applications, such as Word and PowerPoint, in a variety of popular formats to share your results with colleagues;

(15) extended support for image processing and geographic mapping applications through and-on toolboxes.

Notes

[1] MATLAB was originally written to provide easy access to matrix software developed by the LINPACK and EISPACK projects.

　　　　　MATLAB 起初是为了方便使用由 LINPACK 和 EISPACK 项目组开发的矩阵软件而编写的。
　　　　　access to 指有权使用。
　　　　　LINPACK 是 Fortran 语言编写的子程序集，用于解决线性方程和线性最小平方问题。
　　　　　EISPACK 是用 Fortran 语言编写的子程序集，用于解决大规模特征值问题。

[2] With a use community more than 500,000 strong spread throughout industry, government, and academia, MATLAB is the recognized standard worldwide for technical computing.
　　　　　由于有一个多达 50 万以上的用户群广泛分布在工业、政府和学术界，MATLAB 成为工程计算方面世界上公认的标准。
　　　　　strong 和数字连用，意思为"达……之数"。

[3] Using the built-in math and graphics functions and easy-to-use tools, you can analyze and visualize your data on the fly.
　　　　　利用内置的数学和图形函数及易于使用的工具，你可以迅速分析和可视数据。
　　　　　on the fly 指"飞着，急匆匆"，此处引申为"迅速地"。
　　　　　easy-to-use 指"易于使用的"。
　　　　　built-in 指"内部的(嵌入的，固有的)"。

[4] Users working on a broad range of applications with various levels of complexity have found MATLAB to be an effective and flexible environment that grows with them.
　　　　　这是一个复合句，可译为：工作在各种复杂应用场合的用户们发现，MATLAB 是一个有效灵活的环境，能随他们一起发展。
　　　　　a broad range of 指"广泛的"。
　　　　　grow 指"发展或发展并达到成熟"。

[5] ... MATLAB frees engineers and scientists to focus on their real work, avoiding the time-consuming tasks of looking for, developing, debugging, and maintaining homegrown codes.
　　　　　……由于直接内嵌了大量的优化数学程序，MATLAB 使工程师和科

学家能够专注于自己实质性的工作,避免了耗时的寻找、开发、调试及维护代码的工作。

　　develop, debug, maintain 分别意为"开发"、"调试"、"维护"。以上 3 个专业词汇概括了软件开发的整个过程。

　　time-consuming 指"耗费时间的"或"旷日持久的"。

[6] OpenGL

　　OpenGL 是由美国 SGI 公司开发的低层三维图形 API,目前已经成为工业标准,由独立非营利组织 ARB 管理。它在 Windows 中以动态链接库的形式存在,Win95osr2 以上版本及 WinNT 自带有微软公司实现的 OpenGL。

[7] importing common graphical file formats, such as TIFF, JPEG, PNG, BMP, HDF, AVI, and PCX

　　上句包括了通用图形的文件格式,可译为:重要的通用图形文件格式,如 TIFF, JPEG, PNG, BMP, HDF, AVI 和 PCX。

　　PCX：Windows 画笔图像文件。PCX 图像文件最早出现在 Zsoft 公司推出的名叫 PC Paintbrush 的用于绘画的商业软件包中,它是最早支持彩色图像的一种文件格式,最高可达 24 位彩色。PCX 采用行程编码方案对数据进行压缩。

Key words and phrases

matrix	矩阵
intuitive	直觉的
simulation	仿真
built-in	内置的,嵌入的
interactive	交互式的
vector	矢量,向量
matrices	(matrix 的复数)
polynomial	多项式
interpolation	插值;插值法
sparse	稀疏的,稀少的

histogram	直方图
mesh	网格,网孔
triangulated	三角(形)化的;〈拓扑学〉三角部分的
grid	网格,格栅

Exercises

1. Oral practice.

(1) List the key features of MATLAB from the text.
(2) How would you draw a histogram in MATLAB?
(3) Enumerate the common graphical file formats.
(4) What is the original purpose of writing MATLAB?
(5) Why can MATLAB give you immediate access to high-performance numeric computing?
*(6) List some functions in MATLAB for performing mathematical operations and analyzing data.
(7) Briefly describe what is the application of the MATLAB tool in your profession?

2. Translate the following words or phrases into Chinese.

(1) matrix computation
(2) control system design
(3) open architecture
(4) image processing toolbox
(5) earth and life science
(6) structured language
(7) geographic mapping
(8) curve fitting
(9) external routine
(10) I/Q

3. Fill the blanks with the best choice and the correct tense.

interactive	format	algorithm	signal
economic	matrix	vector	written
application	plot	science	engineer

(1) The structured language and programming tools let you save the results of your _____ explorations and develop your own _____ and _____.

(2) The math is optimized for _____ and _____ operations, so you can use it in place of low-level languages like C and C^{++}, with equal performance but less programming.

(3) MATLAB is used in a variety of application areas, including _____ and image processing, control system design, earth and life _____, finance and _____, and instrumentation.

(4) MATLAB includes the specialized graphics in _____ and science.

(5) With MATLAB, you can customize virtually any aspect of your _____ and produce high-equality graphics for _____ and live presentations.

(6) MATLAB imports common graphical file _____, such as TIFF, JPEG, PNG, BMP, HDF, AVI, and PCX.

4. Translate the following words or phrases into English.

(1) 矩阵 (2) 数值积分
(3) 数据采集 (4) 线性代数
(5) 部分分数展开 (6) 嵌入式界面
(7) 奇异值 (8) 稀疏矩阵

5. Write a paragraph, using the following words.

numerical	compute	element	problem	program
introduce	command	select	document	on-line

Extended reading

■ Passage C

FPGAs

Field programmable gate arrays (FPGAs) are digital **integrated circuits** (ICs) that contain configurable (programmable) blocks of logic along with configurabre interconnects between these blocks. Design engineers can configure (program) such devices to perform a tremendous variety of tasks.

Depending on the way in which they are implemented, some FPGAs may only be programmed a single time, while others may be reprogrammed over and over again. Not surprisingly, a device that can be programmed only one time is referred to as being one-time programmable (OTP).

The "field programmable" portion of the FPGA's name refers to the fact that its programming takes place "in the field" (as opposed to devices whose internal functionality is hardwired by the manufacturer). This may mean that FPGAs are configured in the laboratory, or it may refer to modifying the function of a device resident in an electronic system that has already been deployed in the outside world. If a device is capable of being programmed while remaining resident in a higher-level system, it is referred to as being a nin-system programmable (ISP). When it comes to its use, we can use the faces to illustrate.

Today's FPGAs can be used to implement just about anything, including communications devices and software-defined radios (SDR), radar, image, and other digital signal processing (DSP) applications; all the way up to system-on-chip (SOC) components that contain both hardware and software elements.

■ Passage D

VHDL

Very-High-Speed Integrated-Circuit Hardware Description Language (VHDL) is also a general-purpose programming language: just as high-level programming languages allow complex design concepts to be expressed as computer programs, VHDL allows the behavior of complex electronic circuits to be captured into a design system for automatic circuit synthesis or for system simulation. Unlike these other programming languages, VHDL provides features allowing concurrent events to be described. This is important because the hardware described using VHDL is inherently concurrent in its operation.

VHDL is a programming language that has been designed and optimized for describing the behavior of digital systems. VHDL has many features appropriate for describing the behavior of electronic components ranging from simple logic gates to complete microprocessors and custom chips. Features of VHDL allow electrical aspects of circuit behavior (such as rise and fall times of signals, delays through gates, and functional operation) to be precisely described. The resulting VHDL simulation models can then be used as building blocks in larger circuits (using schematics, block diagrams or system-level VHDL descriptions) for the purpose of simulation.

One of the most important applications of VHDL is to capture the performance specification for a circuit, in the form of what is commonly referred to as a test bench. Test benches are VHDL descriptions of circuit stimuli and corresponding expected outputs that verify the behavior of a circuit over time. Test benches should be an integral part of any VHDL project and should be created in random with other descriptions of the circuit.

Key words and phrases

integrated circuits (ICs)	集成电路
in-system programmable(ISP)	在系统内可编程
concurrent	并发的
appropriate	适当的

Application writing

自我介绍

Self-introduction

1. 自我介绍的内容

面试自我介绍时要将自己某些方面的具体情况进行一番自我介绍。这种自我介绍叫作被动型的自我介绍。需高度重视以下几个方面的问题：

（1）控制时间；

（2）讲究态度；

（3）追求真实。

2. 自我介绍的示例

研究生面试自我介绍

Graduate student interview self-introduction

Good afternoon, dear professors. I'm glad to have the opportunity to communicate with professors attending today's interview. First of all, let me briefly introduce myself. My name is ×××, from Guilin, graduating from Gnilin University of Electronic Technology. My major is communication engineering.

I really like this major. During my four-year university life I seriously study the related courses, such as digital circuits, analog circuits, electromagnetic microwave technology, integrated information network, signals and systems, digital signal processing, high frequency electronic circuits, communication principle, optical fiber communication, mobile communication, C language, C++, etc. Our professional practice and further study has laid a solid foundation. Of course I know the importance of this professional practical ability, so I joined our school's students innovative base. I participated in the 2008 National College Students' Mathematical Modeling Competition and the 2009 National Undergraduate Electronic Design Contest. Through the two contests, I learned MATLAB programming and algorithm simulation, the design of hardware circuit PCB, microcontroller development. I have accumulated some SCM development experience, and also improved my ability to cooperate and communicate with people.

I like academic research, hoping to study further in order to obtain the academic career. As for the professional, I'm more interested in signal processing. It has a very important role in our lives, including mobile communications, automatic control, image processing and so on. I think it has a great research value, so I choose it.

I am easy-going. I'm confident, ready to help others, full of the sense of responsibility. I love listening to music, watching movies, reading, playing basketball. If I'm given a chance to continue learning in your university, I will work harder and lay a solid foundation for my future career. I'm looking forward to the beginning of my postgraduate study. Thank you all.

研究生面试自我介绍

各位教授,下午好。很高兴有机会能参加这次面试和各位教授交流。首先,我简洁地介绍一下自己,我叫×××,来自桂林,毕业于电子科技大学,所学的专业是通信工程。

我非常喜欢这个专业。大学四年,我认真学习了与之相关的一些课程,比如数字电路、模拟电路、电磁场微波技术、信息网络集成、信号与系统、数字信号处理、高频电子线路、通信原理、光纤通信、移动通信、C语言、C++等，专业实践和进一步的学习为我打下了坚实的基础。当然，我深知动手实践能力对本专业的重要性，因此我加入了我们学院的大学生创新基地。我参加了2008年全国大学生数学建模大赛和2009年全国大学生电子设计大赛，通过这两次大赛，我学会了MATLAB编程和算法仿真、硬件电路PCB板的设计及单片机开发，积累了一些单片机开发经验，同时也提高了自己与人合作和沟通的能力。

我喜欢学术研究，希望进一步的学习，以期获得学术上的建树。至于专业方面，我对信号处理比较感兴趣，它在我们生活中有着很重要的作用，包括手机通信、自动控制、图像处理等。我认为它具有很大的研究价值，所以我选择它。

我的性格随和。我自信，乐于助人，富有责任心。我爱好听歌，看电影，看书，打篮球。若有机会在贵校学习，我会更加努力，为将来的职业打下坚实的基础。我期待着我研究生学习和生活的开始。谢谢各位。

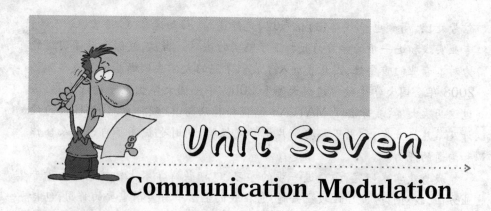

Unit Seven
Communication Modulation

Goals

After studying the unit, you should be able to
- explain the sorts of modulation.
- explain the differences between AM and FM.
- describe the advantages of analog modulation.
- explain the process of modulation and demodulation.
- explain the phenomena when modulation index is bigger, smaller than one.
- judge whether the demodulated waves are distortion.

Texts

■ Passage A

Amplitude, Frequency and Phase Modulation

Usually, the information to be communicated[1] takes the form of a signal, or waveform. The signal might be a speech waveform to be transmitted by radio waves, or a series of pulses representing numbers to be sent over a data telephone line, or a waveform representing the absorption of light by a sample as a function of the wavelength of the light.

It is an interesting fact that a perfectly periodic waveform, such as a sine wave cannot carry any information. For a sine wave to carry information, we must cause the **amplitude**, the frequency, or the **phase** to vary according to the information-carrying waveform. This process is called **modulation**. The inverse process, the recovery of the information waveform from the modulated sinusoid, is called **demodulation**, or **detection**. The sinusoid carrying the information is called the **carrier**, while the waveform of information is often called the modulation.

Let us examine the three basic kinds of modulated waves in more detail. If x is a sinusoidal carrier waveform, we can write:

$$x = A\cos(\omega t + \varphi) \tag{7-1}$$

We will consider three cases: amplitude modulation (AM), in which the amplitude A varies with time; frequency modulation (FM), in which the frequency ω varies with time; or phase modulation (PM), in which the phase φ varies with time.[2] These are illustrated in the following Fig. 7-1.

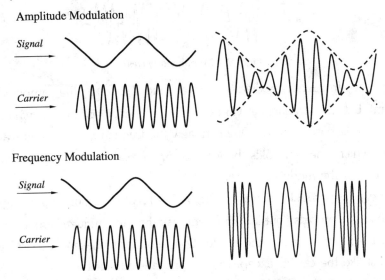

Fig. 7-1　**Amplitude modulation and frequency modulation**

The modulation is the **trapezoidal** wave shown in Fig. 7-2(a), while the carrier is the cosine wave shown in Fig. 7-2(b). In the amplitude modulated case, Fig. 7-2(c), the modulation forms the **envelope** of the modulated carrier. That is, both the positive and negative excursions of the modulated carrier are determined by the magnitude of the modulation waveform. Notice that in the AM case neither the frequency nor the phase of the wave change with time.[3]

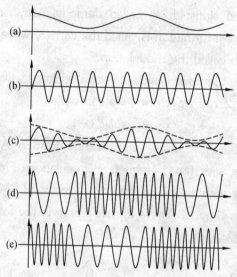

Fig. 7-2 Modulated waves

In the frequency-modulated wave, Fig. 7-2(d), the amplitude is constant but the frequency varies. The frequency is lowest when the modulation is least positive. One can view the frequency-modulated wave as one in which the sinusoids bunch up or spread out according to the magnitude of the modulating wave.

The phase-modulated wave, Fig. 7-2(e), also exhibits bunching and spreading of sinusoids, but in a different way than for frequency modulation. During the flat portions of the modulation (constant phase), the PM wave looks just like the carrier except that its phase is different.

Let a_m be a sinusoidal modulation function

$$a_m = 1 + m\cos\omega_m t \qquad (7\text{-}2)$$

The constant m is called the modulation index. It specifies the fractional variation of the modulation function about its mean value. When this variation is expressed as a percentage, it is called the percent modulation, and is equal to $m \times 100\%$. Waveforms of a_m are plotted in the following Fig. 7-3 for three different choices of m. For $m < 1$, the waveform is always positive. For $m > 1$, the waveform is negative during some portion of a cycle.

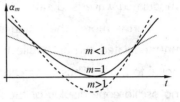

Fig. 7-3 Sinusoidal modulation waveforms

If a wave like a_m is used to modulate the amplitude of a sinusoidal carrier, the waveforms of Fig. 7-4 result.

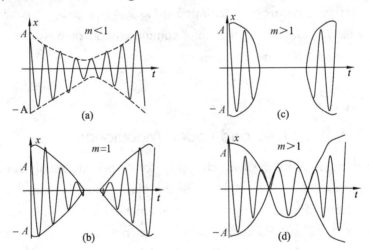

Fig. 7-4 AM waveforms

Assume that the un-modulated carrier is
$$x_c = A\cos\omega_c t \qquad (7\text{-}3)$$
Where
$$\omega_c > \omega_m \qquad (7\text{-}4)$$
The modulated carrier is written
$$x = a_m x_c = A(1 + m\cos\omega_m t)\cos\omega_c t \qquad (7\text{-}5)$$

Consider first $m < 1$, illustrated in Fig. 7-4(a). The envelope of the modulated wave is identical to the modulation waveform.

Furthermore, the mean amplitude is equal to the amplitude A of the un-modulated carrier, while the peak-to-peak excursion of the amplitude is equal to $2mA$. Thus, one can measure the modulation index m directly from no oscilloscope display of the modulated wave.

The value $m = 1$, illustrated in Fig. 7-4(b) is the largest value of m for which the envelope of the modulated wave is equal to the modulation waveform. For $m > 1$, two kinds of situations can arise. Fig. 7-4(c) and (d) illustrate an ideal modulator, in which[4] those portions of the modulation waveform that are negative produce amplitude modulation of the carrier, but which the carrier phase shifted by 180 degrees. A more usual example for the case $m > 1$ is illustrated in Fig. 7-4(c) and (d) is said to be over-modulated. Obviously, if faithful communication of waveforms is the goal, over-modulation must be avoided.

■ Passage B

Pulse and Coded Modulation

Pulse modulation involves changing some parameter of a train of pulses. For example, the amplitude of the pluses could be varied as some function of the information signal $f(t)$. Alternatives would be to vary pulse duration or position. Pulse modulation does not involve a carrier. The resulting modulated signal is still **baseband** but is no longer the original information signal.

Pulse modulation may be classed as **analog** modulation which involves varying the modulated parameter continuously as a linear function of the information signal.[5]

Coded modulation involves changing a characteristic of a pulse train but is a markedly different method from pulse modulation. The method involves first **sampling** the information signal, quantizing the sample by rounding off to the closest of a number of discrete levels, and finally generating a prescribed number of pulses according to a code related to the nearest discrete level. In the simplest system the code may determine the presence or absence of pulse in the prescribed number, or, alternatively, it may determine pulse sign. Both cases correspond to pulses having only two possible levels. More complicated systems are also feasible with pulses having a larger number of discrete levels.

Quantizing and coding amounts to **digitizing** the signal, thus, coded modulation will also be referred to as digital modulation,[6] it is one of the most modern and useful methods of modulation available today.

Notes

[1] the information to be communicated ...

"the information to be communicated ..." 中的 to be communicated 为动词不定式被动结构,作定语,修饰 the information,可译为"信息被传送"。

[2] 本段介绍了模拟调制最基本的 3 种方式,即:AM,振幅调制;PM,相位调制;FM,频率调制。

[3] Notice that in the AM case neither the frequency nor the phase of the wave change with time.

上句给出了幅度调制的一个特点,可译为:值得注意的是,幅度调制波的频率和相位都不会随时间变化而变化。

with time 指"随时间"。

[4] in which

in which = in this case,可译为"在这种情况下"。

[5] Pulse modulation may be classed as analog modulation which involves varying the modulated parameter continuously as a linear function of the information signal.

上句给出了脉冲调制的定义,可译成:脉冲调制可以归结为模拟调制,脉冲调制波包含了连续线性变化的调制参数。

analog modulation：模拟调制　　digital modulation：数字调制
continuously：连续地　　　　　linear：线性的
linear algebra：线性代数

[6] Quantizing and coding amounts to digitizing the signal, thus, coded modulation will also be referred to as digital modulation ...

上句给出了脉冲调制和编码调制的一个区分点,通常通信领域将编码调制视为数字调制,而脉冲调制正如注释[5]所言,可理解为模拟调制。

Key words and phrases

information	信息;(可在计算机中贮存和查找的)数据
waveform	波形
pulse	脉冲
amplitude	振幅;幅度
phase	相位,位相
modulation	调制;调整,调节
demodulation	解调
detection	检测
carrier	载波
trapezoidal	梯形的
envelope	包络
index	指数
over-modulation	过调制
baseband	基带
analog	模拟
sample	取样
digitize	使(数据)数字化

Exercises

1. Oral practice.

(1) What is modulation?
(2) What are the sorts of analog modulation?
(3) What are the sorts of digital modulation?
(4) Explain the differences between amplitude modulation and phase modulation.
(5) When we listen to the radio, it always says: FM 883. Would you please explain the meaning of FM 883?
(6) What is the difference between pulse modulation and coded modulation?

2. We can write wireless electromagnetic wave as the following math expression. Can you point out which is amplitude, frequency or phase?

(1) $V = \cos\omega t$
   Amplitude:
   Frequency:
   Phase:

(2) $V = A\cos\omega t$
   Amplitude:
   Frequency:
   Phase:

(3) $V = A\cos(\omega t + \varphi)$
   Amplitude:
   Frequency:
   Phase:

(4) $V = A\sin(\omega t + \varphi)$
Amplitude：
Frequency：
Phase：

3. Judge the following modulation index whether bigger or less than 1.

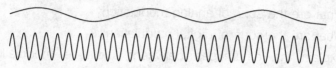

(1)

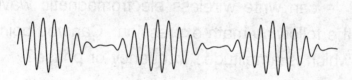

(2)

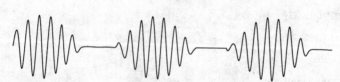

(3)

4. Translate the following sentences or phrases into Chinese.

(1) We will consider three cases: amplitude modulation (AM), in which the amplitude A varies with time; frequency modulation (FM), in which the frequency ω varies with time; or phase modulation (PM), in which the phase φ varies with time.

(2) The constant *m* is called the modulation index. It specifies the fractional variation of the modulation function about its mean value.

(3) speech waveform

(4) data telephone line

(5) information-carrying waveform

(6) trapezoidal wave

(7) percent modulation

(8) peak-to-peak

(9) over modulated

(10) frequency spectrum

5. Translate the following phrases or sentences into English.

(1) 振幅调制

(2) 脉冲调制

(3) 平均功率

(4) 周期信号

(5) 光波长

(6) 一个完善的周期波,例如正弦波,不能携带任何信息。

(7) 每当波形可表示为一系列正弦波的叠加时,各正弦波的振幅可以用所谓频谱形象地显示出来。

(8) 经振幅调制的波的包络线与调制波形相同。

6. Write an essay on the topic "Modulation".

You should write at least 200 words and base your essay on the outline below:

A. Sorts of modulation

B. Why signal needs to be modulated?

C. Introduce at least a modulation manner amply

Extended reading

Passage C

Modulation Benefits and Applications (I)

The primary purpose of modulation in a communication system is to generate a modulated signal suited to the characteristics of the transmission channel. Actually, there are several practical benefits and applications of modulation briefly discussed below.

1. Modulation for efficient transmission

Signal transmission over appreciable distance always involves a traveling electromagnetic wave, with or without a guiding medium, the efficiency of any particular transmission method depends upon the frequency of the signal being transmitted. By exploiting the frequency transition property of CW (Continuous Wave) modulation, message information can be impressed on a carrier whose frequency has been selected for the desired transmission method.

As a case in point, efficient line-of-sight radio propagation requires antennas whose physical dimensions are at least 1/10 of the signal's wavelength. Un-modulated transmission of an audio signal containing frequency components down to 100 Hz would thus call for antennas some 300 km long. Modulated transmission at 100 Hz, as in FM(frequency modulation) broadcasting, allows a practical antenna size of about one meter. At frequency below 100 Hz, other propagation modes have better efficiency with reasonable antenna size.

2. Modulation to overcome hardware limitations

The design of a communication system may be constrained by the cost and availability of hardware, whose performance often depends upon the frequencies involved. Modulation permits the designer to place a signal in some frequency rage that avoids limitations. A particular concern along this line is the question of fractional bandwidth, defined as absolute bandwidth divided by the center frequency. Hardware costs and complications are minimized if the fractional bandwidth is kept within 1% – 10%. Fractional bandwidth considerations account for the fact that modulation units are found in receivers as well as in transmitters.

It likewise follows that signals with large bandwidth should be modulated on high frequency carriers. Since information rate is proportional to bandwidth, according to the Hartley-Shannon law, we conclude that a high information rate requires a high carrier much information in a given time interval as a 500 kHz radio channel. Going even higher in the electromagnetic spectrum, one optical laser beam has a bandwidth potential equivalent to 10 million TV channels.

The following benefits are in the next passage, as Point 3, Point 4 and Point 5.

■ Passage D

Modulation Benefits and Applications (II)

3. Modulation to reduce noise and interference

A brute force method for combating noise and interference is to increase the signal power until it overwhelms the contaminations. But increasing power is costly and may damage equipment. (One of the early transatlantic cables was apparently destroyed by high voltage rupture in an effort to obtain a usable received signal.) Fortunately, FM and certain other types of modulation have the valuable property of suppressing both noise and interference.

This property is called wideband noise reduction because it requires the transmission bandwidth to be much greater than the bandwidth of the modulating signal. Wideband modulation thus allows the designer to exchange increased bandwidth for decreased signal power, a tradeoff implied by the Hartley-Shannon law. Note that a higher carrier frequency may be needed to accommodate wideband modulation.

4. Modulation for frequency assignment

When you tune a radio or television set to a particular station, you are selecting one of the many signals being received at that time. Since each station has a different assigned carrier frequency, the desired signal can be separated from the others by filtering. Were it not for modulation, only one station could broadcast in a given area; otherwise, two or more broadcasting stations would create a hopeless jumble of interference.

5. Modulation for multiplexing

Multiplexing is the process of combining several signals for simultaneous transmission on one channel. Frequency-division multiplexing (FDM) uses CW modulation to put each signal on a different carrier frequency, and a bank of filters separates the signals at the destination. Time-division multiplexing (TDM) uses pulse modulation to put samples of different signals in no-overlapping time slots. For instance, the gaps between pulses could be filled with samples from other signals. A switching circuit at the destination then separates the samples for signal reconstruction.

Applications of multiplexing include data telemetry, FM stereophonic broadcasting, and long-distance telephone. As many as 1,800 voice signals can be multiplexed on a coaxial cable less than one centimeter in diameter. Multiplexing thereby provides another way of increasing communication efficiency.

Key words and phrases

guide	导向,引导
dimension	尺寸
spectrum	频谱
noise	噪声

interference	干涉
tune	调谐
time slot	时隙,时槽
coaxial	同轴的

Application writing

报告
Reports

1. 报告的类型

英文报告主要有以下 4 种类型:

(1) 工作进程报告(the progress report),用来报告某项工作的进展情况。

(2) 定期工作报告(periodic report),往往是以一个周期为主的工作情况汇报。

(3) 调查报告(investigative report),主要记叙对某事或某项工作的调查情况和结果。

(4) 工作建议报告(proposal report),提出建议或对某建议提供论据以表示支持或反对。

2. 报告的格式

英文报告的格式一般有以下几项:

(1) 日期:date

(2) 主题:to

(3) 抄送:cc

(4) 呈报人:from

(5) 事由:reference/subject(re)

3. 报告的示例

工作进程报告

November 20, 2008
To: George Collin, Art Director
　　Dennis Bell, Production Manager
From: Rosa Young, Production Editor
Re: Status & Scheduling, Canadian Financial Accounting

　　To above title, received in manuscript on October 1, has been copy-edited, sent back to author A. I. Rosen for his perusal and further changes, and returned to us on November 15th. The MS was marked up for heads and type, and page format has been decided.

　　Sample type set for us has been checked and then marked, the edited MS was cost-estimated in production and sent out for typesetting. Photographs and artwork now are being discussed. And an approved cover design will be brought to our next meeting.

　　Since the artwork requires more than normal production time for this title, the Art Department has suggested the immediate contracting of a freelance artist. Screens for graphs and tables will have to be discussed and decided before we hire an artist. The art manuscript should also be given immediate attention. So that it can be ready for the typesetter at the same time as the art.

　　We did not discuss the indexing at the last meeting, but since I will be involved with the art manuscript for this title and the copy-editing of two other new manuscripts immediately, and since we expect Rosen's book to run to 985 pages, it is felt that Gerry Smith should be contracted for a freelance indexing job.

　　The cover design should be finalized at our next meeting on the title, and weight the king of material for the cover should be decided.

　　The next meeting for this title is called for Thursday, December 2, 9:30 a.m., in Conference Room B.
　　CC: Marlon Taylor, Special Production Editor
　　　　Barbara Steels, Production Department

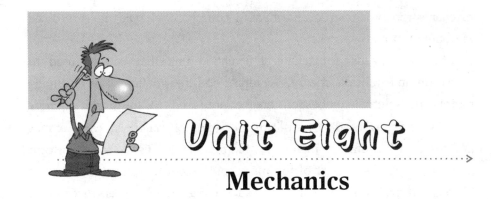

Unit Eight
Mechanics

Goals

After studying the unit, you should be able to
- understand the basic concepts of mechanics.
- comprehend the classification of lathes.

 **Texts**

■ Passage A

Basic Concept in Mechanics

Machinery is a general term of **mechanism** and **machine**.

Mechanism refers to movable devices which can transmit movement and force. The common mechanism involves **tape handler**, **chain-drive mechanism**, gear mechanism, cam mechanism, screw mechanism and so on. [1] These mechanisms generally are considered to be composed by **rigid pipes**. And modern mechanisms may also include the **flexible pipes** and components, such as electric, magnetic, liquid, gas, sound, light and others, in addition to rigid pipes. Therefore, such mechanism is called mechanism in broad sense; mechanism composed of rigid pipes is called mechanism in narrow sense.[2]

Machine means a mechanical actuating unit that can be used to transform and transmit energy, materials and information. For example: motor and internal-combustion engine are used to transform energy; machine tools are used to transform the status of materials; cars, cranes are used to transfer materials; computer is used to transform information.[3] As a result of the main component of various machines is various mechanisms, it can be said that a machine is mechanism combination used to transform or transmit energy, materials and information. They can be divided into two categories according to their uses: all those which convert energy of other forms to mechanical energy are called prime mover; those complete the effective work using mechanical energy are called working machine.[4]

The basic theory of machinery is as follows:

1. Structure analysis of mechanism
(1) Study what is the composition of mechanism, and its impact on the movement, as well as the conditions of its determination for movement.
(2) Study the principle of mechanism composition and the types.
(3) Learn how to draw schematic diagram of mechanism movement.

2. Motion analysis of mechanism

Introduce the basic motion analysis principles and methods of mechanism (including analysis of displacement, velocity and acceleration).

3. Machine dynamics

Analyse the forces of components when machines are running, as well as the working station of these forces.

4. Analysis and design of common mechanism

Study the type, operational principle and motion characteristics analysis of common mechanism (such as link mechanism, cam mechanism, gear mechanism, etc.). Study the basic principles and methods of common mechanism design.

5. Motion conceptual design of mechanical drive system

Study mechanical selection, combination and variation during the specific design. Study the motion conceptual design of mechanical drive system, and so on.

■ Passage B

Lathes

Lathes (shown in Fig. 8-1) are widely used in industry to produce all kinds of machined parts. Some are general-purpose machines, and others are used to perform highly specialized operations.

Fig. 8-1 Example of a lathe

1. Engine lathes

Engine lathes, of course, are general-purpose machines used in production and maintenance shops all over the world.[5] Sizes range from small bench models to huge **heavy-duty** pieces of equipment. Many of the larger lathes come equipped with **attachments** not commonly found in the ordinary shop, such as automatic stops for the carriage.

2. Tracer or duplicating lathes

The tracer or duplicating lathe is designed to produce irregularly shaped parts automatically. The basic operation of this lathe is as follows. A template of either a flat or three-dimensional shape is placed in a holder. A guide or pointer then moves along this shape and its movement controls that of the cutting tool.[6] The duplication may include a square or tapered shoulder, grooves, tapers, and contours. Work such as motor shafts, spindles, pistons, rods, car axles, turbine shafts, and a variety of other objects can be turned using this type of lathe.[7]

3. Turret lathes

When machining a complex workpiece on a general-purpose lathe, a great deal of time is spent changing and adjusting the several tools that are needed to complete the work.[8] One of the first adaptations of the engine lathe which made it more suitable to mass production was the addition of multi-tool turret in place of the tailstock. Although most turrets have six stations, some have as many as eight.

4. Automatic screw machines

Screw machines are similar in construction to turret lathes, except that their heads are designed to hold and feed long bars of stock. Otherwise, there is little difference between them. Both are designed for multiple tooling, and both have adaptations for identical work. Originally, the turret lathe was designed as a chucking lathe for machining small castings, forgings, and irregularly shaped workpieces.

The first screw machines were designed to feed bar stock and wire used in making small screw parts. Today, however, the turret lathe is frequently used with a collet attachment, and the automatic screw machine can be equipped with a chuck to hold castings.

5. Vertical turret lathes

A vertical turret lathe is basically a turret lathe that has been stood on its headstock end. It is designed to perform a variety of turning operations. It consists of a turret, a **revolving table**, and a side head with a **square turret** for holding additional tools. Operations performed by any of the tools mounted on the turret or side head can be controlled through the use of stops.

6. Machining centers

Many of today's more sophisticated lathes are called machining centers since they are capable of performing, in addition to the normal turning operations, certain milling and **drilling** operations.[9] Basically, a machining center can be thought to be a combination of turret lathes and milling machines. Additional features are sometimes included by manufacturers to increase the versatility of their machines.

Notes

[1] Mechanism refers to movable devices which can transmit movement and force. The common mechanism involves tape handler, chain-drive mechanism, gear mechanism, cam mechanism, screw mechanism and so on.

　　机构是指一种用来传递运动和力的可动装置。常见的机构有带传动机构、链传动机构、齿轮机构、凸轮机构、螺旋机构等。

[2] And modern mechanisms may also include the flexible pipes and components, such as electric, magnetic, liquid, gas, sound, light and others, in addition to rigid pipes. Therefore, such mechanism is called mechanism in broad sense; mechanism composed of rigid pipes is called mechanism in narrow sense.

　　而现代机构中除了刚性管以外，还可能有弹性管和电、磁、液、气、声、光等元件。故这类机构称为广义机构，而由刚性管组成的机构就称为狭义机构。

[3] For example: motor and internal-combustion engine are used to transform energy; machine tools are used to transform the status of materials; cars, cranes are used to transfer materials; computer is

used to transform information.

例如，电动机、内燃机用来变换能量，机床用来变换物料的状态，汽车、起重机用来传递物料，计算机用来变换信息。

[4] They can be divided into two categories according to their uses: all those which convert energy of other forms to mechanical energy are called prime mover; those complete the effective work using mechanical energy are called working machine.

机器按其用途可分为两类：凡将其他形式的能量转换为机械能的机器称为原动机，凡利用机械能来完成有用功的机器称为工作机。

[5] Engine lathes, of course, are general-purpose machines used in production and maintenance shops all over the world.

普通车床是全世界的生产车间和维修车间里广泛使用的通用机床。

[6] The basic operation of this lathe is as follows. A template of either a flat or three-dimensional shape is placed in a holder. A guide or pointer then moves along this shape and its movement controls that of the cutting tool.

这种车床的基本操作如下：在夹持装置上安装平面或立体形状的样板，然后，导向触头或指针沿着它的外形移动，从而控制切削刀具的运动。

[7] Work such as motor shafts, spindles, pistons, rods, car axles, turbine shafts, and a variety of other objects can be turned using this type of lathe.

像电动机的轴、主轴、活塞、杆件、汽车轴、汽轮机轴和其他很多种类的工件都可以采用这种车床来进行切削加工。

[8] When machining a complex workpiece on a general-purpose lathe, a great deal of time is spent changing and adjusting the several tools that are needed to complete the work.

在通用车床上加工一个复杂的工件时，在更换和调整加工时所用的一些刀具上要花费很多时间。

[9] Many of today's more sophisticated lathes are called machining centers since they are capable of performing, in addition to the

normal turning operations, certain milling and drilling operations.
　　当前,许多技术更为先进的精密车床叫作机床中心。因为,它们除了完成常规的车削工序之外,还可以完成某些铣削、钻削工序。

Key words and phrases

machinery	机械
mechanism	结构;机构
tape handler	带传动机构
chain-drive mechanism	链传动机构
gear mechanism	齿轮机构
cam mechanism	凸轮机构
screw mechanism	螺旋机构
rigid pipe	刚性管
flexible pipe	软管,挠性管
internal-combustion engine	内燃机
prime mover	原动机
working machine	工作机
lathe	车床
engine lathe	普通车床
heavy-duty	重型的;重载的;耐用的;高功率的
attachment	附件,附属装置
automatic stop	自动止动器,自动止动装置
carriage	(机床的)拖板,溜板
tracer or duplicating lathe	靠模车床或仿形车床

template	样板，模板
holder	夹持装置，固定器
tapered	锥形的
shoulder	（机械的）肩形凸出部，台肩，凸头
groove	凹槽，沟
contour	轮廓，形状，外形
work	工件
automatic screw machine	自动螺丝车床
turret lathe	六角（转塔）车床
tooling	机床安装，刀具加工
chucking lathe	卡盘车床
casting	铸件
forging	锻件
bar stock	棒材，型材
collet	夹头，有缝夹套
vertical turret lathe	立式六角（转塔）车床
revolving table	旋转工作台
square turret	（车床的）四方六角（转塔）刀架，四方刀架
mount	安装，固定
drilling	钻孔

Exercises

1. Oral practice.

What do you know about machinery?

2. Put the following phrases into English.

(1) 机械　　　　　　　　(2) 链传动机构
(3) 凸轮机构　　　　　　(4) 齿轮机构
(5) 刚性管　　　　　　　(6) 软管
(7) (机床的)拖板,溜板　　(8) 原动机
(9) 工件　　　　　　　　(10) 铸件
(11) 锻件　　　　　　　　(12) 钻孔
(13) 六角(转塔)车床　　　(14) 机床安装,刀具加工
(15) 立式六角(转塔)车床　(16) 旋转工作台

3. Translate the following sentences into Chinese or English.

(1) 研究常用机构(如连杆机构、凸轮机构、齿轮机构等)的类型、工作原理及运动特性分析和机构设计的基本原理及方法。

(2) 研究在进行具体机械设计时机构的选型、组合、变异及机械传动系统运动方案的设计等问题。

(3) Lathes (shown in Fig. 8-1) are widely used in industry to produce all kinds of machined parts. Some are general-purpose machines, and others are used to perform highly specialized operations.

(4) Many of the larger lathes come equipped with attachments not commonly found in the ordinary shop, such as automatic stops for the carriage.

(5) Screw machines are similar in construction to turret lathes, except that their heads are designed to hold and feed long bars of stock.

(6) It consists of a turret, a revolving table, and a side head with a square turret for holding additional tools.

4. Writing.

Please write an invitation letter to invite your classmates to your birthday party.

Extended reading

■ Passage C

Lathe Cutting Tools

The shape and geometry of the lathe tools depend upon the purpose for which they are employed. Turning tools can be classified into two main groups, namely, external cutting tools and internal cutting tools. Each of these two groups includes the following types of tools.

Turning tools. Turning tools can be either finishing or rough turning tools. Rough turning tools have small nose radii and are employed when deep cuts are made. On the other hand, finishing tools have larger nose radii and are used for obtaining the final required dimensions with good surface finished by making slight depths of cut. Rough turning tools can be right-hand or left-hand type, depending upon the direction of feed. They can have straight, bent, or offset shanks.

Facing tools. Facing tools are employed in facing operations for machining plane-side or end surfaces. There are tools for machining left-hand-side surfaces and tools for right-hand-side surfaces. Those side surfaces are generated through the use of the cross feed, contrary to turning operations, where the usual longitudinal feed is used.

Cutoff tools. Cutoff tools, which are sometimes called parting tools, serve to separate the workpiece into parts and/or machine external annular grooves.

Thread-cutting tools. Thread-cutting tools have either triangular, square, or trapezoidal cutting edges, depending upon the cross section of the desired thread. Also, the plane angles of these tools must always be identical to those of the thread forms. Thread-cutting tools have straight shanks for external thread cutting and are of the bent-shank type when cutting internal threads.

Form tools. Form tools have edges especially manufactured to take a certain form, which is opposite to the desired shape of the machined workpiece. An HSS(High-speed Steel) tool is usually made in the form of a single piece, contrary to cemented carbides or ceramic cemented carbides, which are made in the form of tips. The latter are brazed or mechanically fastened to steel shanks.

■ Passage D

Shafts and Couplings

Virtually all machines contain shafts. The most common shape for shafts is circular and the cross section can be either solid or hollow (hollow shafts can result in weight savings). Rectangular shafts are sometimes used, as in screwdriver blades, socket wrenches and control knob stems.

A shaft must have adequate torsional strength to transmit torque and not be over stressed. It must also be torsionally stiff enough so that one mounted component does not deviate excessively from its original angular position relative to a second component mounted on the same shaft. Generally speaking, the angle of twist should not exceed one degree in a shaft length equal to 20 diameters.

Shafts are mounted in bearings and transmit power through such devices as gears, pulleys, cams and clutches. These devices introduce forces which attempt to bend the shaft; hence, the shaft must be rigid enough to prevent overloading of the supporting bearings. In general, the bending deflection of a shaft should not exceed 0.01 in. per ft of length between bearing supports.

In addition, the shaft must be able to sustain a combination of bending and torsional loads. Thus an equivalent load must be considered which takes into account both torsion and bending. Also, the allowable stress must contain a factor of safety which includes fatigue, since torsional and bending stress reversals occur.

Components such as gears and pulleys are mounted on shafts by means of key. The design of the key and the corresponding keyway in the shaft must be properly evaluated. For example, stress concentrations occur in shafts due to keyways, and the material removed to form the keyway further weakens the shaft.

Another important aspect of shaft design is the method of directly connecting one shaft to another. This is accomplished by devices such as rigid and flexible couplings.

A coupling is a device for connecting the ends of adjacent shafts. In machine construction, couplings are used to effect a semipermanent connection between adjacent rotating shafts. The connection is permanent in the sense that it is not meant to be broken during the useful life of the machine, but it can be broken and restored in an emergency or when worn parts are replaced.

There are several types of shaft couplings, their characteristics depend on the purpose for which they are used. If an exceptionally long shaft is required in a manufacturing plant or a propeller shaft on a ship, it is made in sections that are coupled together with rigid couplings. A common type of rigid coupling consists of two mating radial flanges (disks) that are attached by key driven hubs to the ends of adjacent shaft sections and bolted together through the flanges to form a rigid connection. Alignment of the connected shafts is usually effected by means of a rabbet joint on the face of the flanges.

Application writing

邀请信
Invitation

邀请信是邀请亲朋好友或知名人士、专家等参加某项活动时所发的约请性书信。在国际交往及日常的各种社交活动中,这类书信使用广泛,一般包括宴会、舞会、晚餐、聚会、婚礼等各种邀请信件。形式上大体分为两种:一种为正规的格式(formal correspondence),亦称请柬;一种是非正式格式(informal correspondence),即一般的邀请信。一般的邀请信在形式上不如请柬那样正规,但也很考究。

1. 邀请信的格式

邀请信的基本格式主要由5个部分组成:

(1)初步的细节,例如发件人的地址和日期,收件人的姓名、地址,以及问候。

(2)介绍你自己或你的组织的打算。

(3)描述活动的性质和目的,提供一切必要的细节。你也可以指明被邀请人是否需要携带特定物品,或者在活动中担任特殊角色。你还应该提到需要答复的特定日期。

(4)用一句简短的话表明希望宾客出席或期待他们的最终答复。

(5)做正式或非正式的签字,这取决于邀请函的性质。

注意:邀请信尽量简洁明了,看懂就行,文字不宜太多。无论是正式或非正式的邀请函,书写时要将邀请的时间(年、月、日、钟点)、地点、场合写清楚,不能使接信人存在任何疑虑。

2. 邀请信的复信

邀请信的复信要求简明扼要,在书写时应注意以下几点:

(1)接受邀请的复信中应重复写上邀请信中的某些内容,如邀请年、月、日、星期几、几点钟等。

(2)邀请信的复信中应明确表明接受邀请还是不接受邀请,不能含糊其辞,使对方无法做出相应安排。在接受邀请的复信中,应对受到邀请表示高兴;谢绝的复信中应阐明不能应邀的缘由。

3. 邀请信的示例

邀请朋友同他们不认识的人一起共进晚餐

Inviting friends to dinner with strangers

Dear Susan,

  I know you are interested in oil painting, so I'm sure you'll be interested in Mr. and Mrs. Lin Dun! They are coming here to supper next Sunday night, October the twelfth, and we'd like you and Walter to come, too.

  Mr. and Mrs. Lin Dun are that very charming couple we met in London last summer. They have a wonderful collection of oil paintings of various stages; and I understand that Mr. Lin Dun is quite an authority on oil painting. I'm sure you and Walter will thoroughly enjoy the evening in their company.

  We're planning supper at six, which will give us a nice long evening to talk. If I don't hear from you before then, I'll be expecting you on the twelfth!

Affectionately yours,
Li Ming

4. 邀请信复信的示例

（1）接受邀请

Dear Li Ming,

  I'll be delighted to come to your dinner on Sunday night, October the twelfth, at six o'clock.

  I am so happy to communicate with such an authority on oil painting. I assure it will be a nice night. Thank you so much for inviting me.

Truly yours,
Susan

(2) 辞谢邀请

Dear Li Ming,

    I am very grateful to you for inviting me to your supper. And I also would like to communicate with Mr. and Mrs. Lin Dun. But unfortunately I expect guests myself on Sunday night, October the twelfth; and therefore cannot accept your invitation on that day.

    It was thoughtful of you to invite me, and I am extremely sorry I cannot accept. I do hope you will ask me again some time!

Sincerely yours,
Susan

Unit Nine
Automobile

Goals

After studying this unit, you should be able to

- describe the stages of development process of automobiles.
- describe the symbols and allusions of automobiles.
- describe the basic structure of an automobile and explain its functions.
- follow some guidelines before purchasing a new automobile.
- read and translate the information about automobiles in English.

Texts

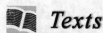 Passage A

The Birth of Automobiles

The history of the **automobile** actually began about 4,000 years ago when the first wheel was used for transportation in India. Several Italians recorded designs for wind-driven vehicles. The first was Guido da Vigevano in 1335. It was a windmill-type drive to gears and thus to wheels. Later Leonardo da Vinci designed clockwork-driven tricycle with tiller steering and a differential mechanism between the rear wheels.[1]

In the early 15th century, the Portuguese arrived in China and the interaction of the two cultures led to a variety of new technologies, including the creation of a wheel that turned under its own power. By the 1600s, small steam-powered engine models were developed.

A Catholic priest named Father Ferdinan Verbiest is credited to have built a steam-powered vehicle for the Chinese Emperor Qianlong in about 1678. There is no information about the vehicle, only the event. James Watt didn't invent the steam engine until 1705.

Although by the mid-15th century the idea of a self-propelled vehicle had been put into practice with the development of experimental vehicles powered by means of springs, clockworks, and the wind, Nicolas-Joseph Cugnot of France is considered to have built the first true automobile in 1769. Designed by Cugnot and constructed by M. Brezin, it was also the first vehicle to move under its own power for which there is a record. Cugnot's three-wheeled steam-powered vehicle carried four persons. It had a top speed of a little more than 3.2 km/h (about 2 mph).

Evans was the first American who obtained a patent for "a self-propelled carriage". He, in fact, attempted to create a two-in-one combination of a steam wagon and a flat-bottomed boat, which didn't receive any attention in those days. During the 1830s, the steam vehicle had made great advances. But stiff competition from railway companies and legislations in Britain forced the poor steam vehicle gradually out of use on roads. The early steam-powered vehicles were so heavy that they were only practical on a perfectly flat surface as strong as iron. A road thus made out of iron rails became the norm of the next hundred and twenty-five years. The vehicle got bigger and heavier and more powerful and they were eventually capable of pulling a train of many cars filled with freight and passengers.

Karl Friedrich Benz and Gottlieb Daimler, both Germans, share the credit of changing the transport habits of the world, for their efforts laid the foundation of the great motor industry as we know it today. First, Benz invented the **petrol engine** in 1885 and a year later Daimler made a car driven by motor of his own design.

Daimler's engine proved to be a great success because of its less weight that could deliver 1,000 rpm (revolution per minute) and needed only very small and light vehicles to carry them.[2]

France too had joined the motoring scenario by 1890 when two Frenchmen Panhard and Levassor began producing vehicles powered by Daimler's engine, and Daimler himself, **possessed** by the automobile spirit, went on adding new features to his engine. He built the first V-Twin engine with a glowing platinum tube to explode the cylinder gas—the very earliest form of a **sparking plug**.[3]

For many years after the introduction of automobiles, three kinds of power sources were in common use: steam engines, gasoline or petrol engines, and electric motors.[4] In 1900, over 2,300 automobiles were registered in New York, Boston, Massachusetts, and Chicago. Of these, 1,170 were steam cars, 800 were electric cars, and only 400 were gasoline cars.

In ten years from the invention of the petrol engine, the motorcar had evolved itself into **amazing** designs and shapes. By 1898, there were 50 automobile-manufacturing companies in the United States, a number that rose to 241 by 1908. In that year, Henry Ford revolutionized the manufacture of automobiles with his assembly-line style of production and brought out the Model T, a car that was inexpensive, versatile, and easy to **maintain**. The introduction of the Model T transformed the automobile from a plaything of the rich to an item that even people of modest income could afford; by the late 1920s the car was commonplace in modern industrial nations.

Automobile manufacturers in the 1930s and 1940s **refined** and improved on the principles of Ford and other pioneers. Cars were generally large, and many were still extremely expensive and luxurious; many of the most collectible cars date from this time. The increased affluence of the United States after World War II led to the development of large cars, while most companies in Europe made smaller, more fuel-efficient cars. Since the mid-1970s, the rising cost of fuel has increased the demand for these smaller cars, many of which have been produced in Japan as well as in Europe and the United States.[5]

Notes

[1] Later Leonardo da Vinci designed clockwork-driven tricycle with tiller steering and a differential mechanism between the rear wheels.

后来,列奥纳多·达·芬奇(Leonardo da Vinci)设计了齿轮与发条装置驱动的三轮车,带有舵柄转向装置和后轮之间的差速器。

[2] Daimler's engine proved to be a great success because of its less weight that could deliver 1,000 rpm (revolution per minute) and needed only very small and light vehicles to carry them.

戴姆勒的发动机被认为是一项伟大的成就,因为它的重量更轻,能输出每分钟1 000 转的转速,只需非常小而轻的车辆来承载它们。

[3] He built the first V-Twin engine with a glowing platinum tube to explode the cylinder gas—the very earliest form of a sparking plug.

他造出了第一台 V 型双列发动机,装有使气缸气体爆发的白金管——早期形式的火花塞。

[4] For many years after the introduction of automobiles, three kinds of power sources were in common use: steam engines, gasoline or petrol engines, and electric motors.

在汽车使用之后很多年,三种动力源被普遍应用:蒸汽发动机、汽油发动机及电动发动机。

[5] Since the mid-1970s, the rising cost of fuel has increased the demand for these smaller cars, many of which have been produced

in Japan as well as in Europe and the United States.

自20世纪70年代中期始,燃油价格的上涨增加了这些小型汽车的需求量,许多这样的小型汽车是在日本、欧洲和美国生产的。

Key words and phrases

automobile	汽车
windmill	风车,磨坊;(通过转动将风能转化为电能的风车)
mechanism	机械装置,机件;机制
differential mechanism	差速器
interaction	相互作用;交流
practice	实践,实际行动
propel	推动,推进;驱使
experimental	以实验为基础的,实验性的
freight	货物,货运
petrol	〈英〉汽油
possessed	(~by sth) 对……入迷
sparking plug	火花塞
amazing	令人惊奇的
maintain	维持;维修
refine	精炼,提纯
collectible	值得收藏(或收集、采集)的

Exercises

1. Answer the following questions.

(1) When did the history of the automobile actually begin?

(2) Who is considered to have built the first true automobile in 1769?

(3) Why were the early steam-powered vehicles only practical on a perfectly flat surface as strong as iron?

(4) Who built the first V-Twin engine with a glowing platinum tube to explode the cylinder gas—the very earliest form of a sparking plug?

(5) Why has the demand for these smaller cars increased since the mid-1970s?

2. Translate following expressions into English.

(1) 差速器

(2) 火花塞

(3) 自动驱动汽车

(4) V 型双列发动机

(5) 汽油发动机

(6) 现代工业国家

3. Translate following sentences into English.

(1) 17 世纪初,小型蒸汽动力发动机出现了。

(2) 1885 年,卡尔·奔驰发明了汽油发动机。

(3) 戴姆勒为汽车的活力而着魔,想要为他的发动机注入新的特色。

(4) 汽车是便宜的,多功能的,易于维修的。

(5) 20 世纪 20 年代,汽车在现代工业国家成为平常事物。

(6) 二战之后美国的新富开始发展大汽车。

4. Study the following list and name.

(1) two-door sedan, four-door sedan, fixed head coupe, hard-top sedan, limousine, station wagon, drophead coupe, convertible, sports car, minicar, jeep, field vehicle

(2) bus, omnibus, service vehicle, coach, luxury coach, touring bus, articulated bus, double-deck bus, passenger-trailer,

minibus, microbus, articulated trolleybus

(3) lorry, truck, high-way vehicle, board truck, canvas top, box-van truck, van, electromabil, delivery van, pick-up, cargobus, general-purpose truck, multipurpose vehicle, short-wheelbase truck

(4) rear dump, side tipper, container carrier, tank-truck, bulk truck, thermos van, refrigerated vehicle, furniture van

Passage B

Basic Structure of an Automobile

Today's average automobile contains more than 15,000 separate parts that they must work together. Automobiles are basically the same in structure, although they are quite different in style and design. In other words, any automobile is composed of four sections, such as the **engine**, the chassis, the car body and the **electric** system (see Fig. 9-1).[1]

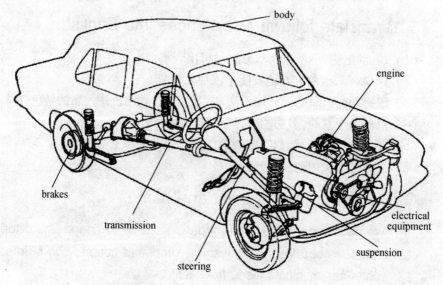

Fig. 9-1 Layout of an automobile

Among them, the engine is the power source that makes a car move.

There are two kinds of engines in use: gasoline engines and diesel engines. The burning of the fuel inside an engine produces high pressure in the engine's combustion chamber. This high pressure forces pistons to move, which is carried by connecting rods to the crankshaft. [2] The crankshaft is thus made to rotate, the rotary motion is delivered through the power train to the driving wheels and then the car moves. It includes crankshaft connecting rod system, valve mechanism, fuel supply system, cooling and lubricating system, starting system and ignition system.

The chassis acts as the base of an automobile to support other parts equipped on the vehicle. It includes the transmission system, the running device, the steering and the brake system.

The transmission system is installed between the engine and the driving wheels. It is a device which can change speed and power, and can transfer the output torque of an engine to driving wheels. [3] The two types of transmission are manual transmission, which the driver shifts by hand, and automatic transmission, which shifts automatically.

The running device is the foundation of an auto. It includes the frame, the axle, wheels and tires.

The suspension system is installed between the frame and the axle. The suspension supports the weight of the vehicle, absorbs road shocks, transmits brake-reaction forces, helps maintain traction between the tires and the road. [4] The springs may be coil, leaf, torsion bar, or air. Most automotive vehicles have coil springs at the front and either coil or leaf springs at the rear.

The steering system is used to control the driving direction, which can be manual or power-assisted. [5] Steering systems are classified as either manual steering or power steering, with power assist provided hydraulically or by an electric motor.

A brake system is composed of the brake and its control mechanisms. A brake is a device that uses a controlled force to reduce the speed or to stop a moving vehicle, or to hold the vehicle stationary. There are two kinds of brake systems: service brake systems and parking brake systems.

The car body is the structure used to protect the driver, passengers and cargos. The body of a heavy truck consists of the cab and its packing case, while the body of a couch or a car is made up of car crust; other special vehicles have some other special devices. Car body also includes these devices like doors, windows, chairs, external or internal gadgets, and other accessories.

The electric system is composed of electric power and electrical devices, such as the air-conditioning system, windshield wipers, the clock, defogger, fog lamps, fuel injectors, gauges, headlights, ignition, cigar lighter, power windows, horn, and power seats and so on.

Notes

[1] In other words, any automobile is composed of four sections, such as the engine, the chassis, the car body and the electric system.

换句话说,任何汽车都由4部分组成:发动机、底盘、车身和电气系统。

[2] The burning of the fuel inside an engine produces high pressure in the engine's combustion chamber. This high pressure forces pistons to move, which is carried by connecting rods to the crankshaft.

发动机内的燃料在发动机燃烧室中燃烧产生了高压力。这种高压力驱动活塞运动,这种运动通过曲柄连杆机构传递。

[3] It is a device which can change speed and power, and can transfer the output torque of an engine to driving wheels.

这是一个可以改变速度和功率的装置,可以把发动机输出的转矩传递到驱动轮。

[4] The suspension supports the weight of the vehicle, absorbs road shocks, transmits brake-reaction forces, helps maintain traction between the tires and the road.

悬挂支撑车辆的重量,吸收路面震动,传输制动反应力,有助于保持轮胎与路面之间的附着摩擦力。

[5] The steering system is used to control the driving direction, which can be manual or power-assisted.

转向系统是用来控制行驶方向,可通过手动转向或动力转向。

Key words and phrases

structure	构造
engine	发动机
chassis	(车辆的)底盘;底座
electric	电的;电动的
crankshaft	曲轴,曲柄轴
rotary	旋转的,绕轴转动的
transmission	(车辆的)变速器;传动装置
ignition	点燃,点火
suspension	(车辆减震用的)悬架
install	安装,设置
torque	(使机器等旋转的)转矩
classify	将……分类,将……归类
cargo	(船或飞机装载的)货物
be composed of	由……构成
electric system	电气系统
gasoline engine	汽油发动机
diesel engine	柴油发动机
combustion chamber	燃烧室
crankshaft connecting rod system	曲轴连杆系统
valve mechanism	气门机构
fuel supply system	燃料供给系统
cooling and lubricating system	冷却和润滑系统

starting system and ignition system	启动系统和点火系统
transmission system	传动系统
running device	行驶装置
steering system	转向系统
brake system	制动系统
suspension system	悬挂系统

Exercises

1. **Read and judge.** Read the passage and judge whether the statement is T(true) or F(false).

( ) (1) Different vehicles have different basic structures.
( ) (2) A crankshaft is the power source that makes a car move.
( ) (3) The chassis is the structure to support other parts of a car.
( ) (4) The body of different models of vehicle is different.
( ) (5) Electric devices belong to the electric system.

2. **Read, complete and retell.** Read the passage again and fill in the blanks with the information in the passage, and then try to retell the passage.

An automobile consists of four basic mechanisms: _____, _____, _____, and _____. The engine is the power source that makes a car move. There are two kinds of engines in use: _____ engines and _____ engines. The chassis acts as the _____ for an automobile to support other parts equipped on the vehicle. It includes the transmission system, the running device, the steering and the _____. The car body is the structure used to protect the driver, passengers and cargos. The electric system is composed of _____ and _____.

3. Revise and Translate. Translate the following sentences into Chinese.

(1) Commonly an automobile consists of four basic mechanisms no matter different models and different manufacturers: the engine, the chassis, the car body and its accessories, and the electric system.
(2) The engine is the power source that makes a car move.
(3) The chassis acts as the base of an automobile to support other parts equipped on the vehicle.
(4) The car body is the structure used to protect the driver, passengers and cargos.
(5) The electric system is composed of electric power and electrical devices.

 Extended reading

■ Passage C

Automobile Purchase

The history of the automobile is the history of an evolution — approximately 100,000 patents are responsible for the modern automobile.

• Nicolas Cugnot was credited with the first creation of a car in 1769. 1807 saw the development of the internal combustion engine.

• Nikolas August Otto came up with the four-stroke engine in 1876. Karl Benz was credited with building the world's first practical automobile to be powered by an internal combustion engine in 1885.

• Henry Ford then improved the assembly line for automobile manufacturing.

• Later, Rudolf Diesel invented the diesel-fueled internal combustion engine.

This pioneering age of automobiles played a vital role in building the foundation of automotive technology. The speed and power of an automobile gave vent to man's competitive nature and motor sports became popular. This, in turn, brought about astounding improvements in speed performance in automobiles.[1] Gradually, luxury automobile models were being developed. In the early 1900s, American automobile companies were ruling the roost. Japanese Government enacted the Automobile Manufacturing Act in the 1930s to increase its domestic automobile production and improve its trade balance with the United States.[2] In the 50 years or so that followed, Japanese automotive technology made remarkable progress. Japan came to being recognized as a top automobile-manufacturing country. The future of the automobile industry in the new millennium depends on usage of high-tech electronics, new power sources and artificial intelligence.

You need to follow some guidelines before buying a new automobile. Listed below are a few pointers towards buying a new automobile:

- Decide on the kind of car you need.
- Fix on an approximate budget.[3]
- Consider the options of leasing or buying a new automobile.
- Do a thorough automobile comparison in terms of features and automobile pricing.
- Test-drive the car that you have firmed up on.

Automobile purchase involves careful selection between different makes and models. An automobile comparison must be made to find out the one that suits your needs best. An automobile comparison will show you the different categories of passenger vehicles: convertible / coupe / hatchback / minivan / sedan / SUV / van /wagon.[4]

While buying an automobile, you can take the services of an automobile purchase advisory firm. Read and peruse all documents carefully. Back-up service and parts availability are also to be considered while going in for automobile purchase.

The Automobile Blue Book offers suggested **retail** values on a wide range of vehicles. You can look up the Automobile Blue Book value of a base vehicle with no optional equipment or even the top-of-the-line engine model. An Automobile Blue Book value gives ratings of excellent, good, fair and poor to automobiles based on certain **criteria**.

Excellent rating: This automobile rating indicates that the vehicle is in excellent mechanical condition and has passed **the smog test**. **Glossy** painted body, proper tires, clean title and automobile history are requisites for an excellent automobile rating. [5]

Good rating: A good automobile rating shows that the vehicle is **sans** major defects. Most used cars fall in this category. Minor **blemishes** in paint, body and interior coupled with no major mechanical problems qualify for a good automobile rating. [5]

Fair rating: When an automobile gets a fair rating, it is likely that the vehicle has some mechanical defects but is in decent running condition. Replacement of tires and paint and bodywork may be required. A fair automobile rating assumes a clean automobile history. Many a time, even after significant reconditioning, the automobile may not qualify for an Automobile Blue Book value. [6]

Poor rating: The Automobile Blue Book value of such vehicles is generally not listed.

Notes

[1] The speed and power of an automobile gave vent to man's competitive nature and motor sports became popular. This, in turn, brought about astounding improvements in speed performance in automobiles.

汽车的速度和动力为人类的竞争本性找到了发泄点,使得汽车运动变得普及起来。因此,这为汽车的速度性能带来了令人惊奇的进步。

[2] Japanese Government enacted the Automobile Manufacturing Act in the 1930s to increase its domestic automobile production and improve its trade balance with the United States.

20世纪30年代,日本政府颁布《汽车制造业法》,以增加国产汽车生产,并改善与美国的国际贸易差额。

[3] Fix on an approximate budget.

做一个大概的预算。

[4] An automobile comparison will show you the different categories of passenger vehicles: convertible/coupe/hatchback/minivan/sedan/SUV/van/wagon.

通过挑选汽车,你会看到不同的汽车种类:活动顶篷式汽车、双门小汽车、掀背式汽车、小型面包车、(三厢)四门轿车、SUV、客货车、货车。

[5] Glossy painted body, proper tires, clean title and automobile history are requisites for an excellent automobile rating.

对于一辆极佳级别的汽车来说,平滑光亮的车身油漆、原配轮胎、清晰的所有权和汽车来历是必不可少的。

[6] Many a time, even after significant reconditioning, the automobile may not qualify for an Automobile Blue Book value.

即使经过多次的,甚至是重大维修之后,汽车也可能没资格跻身于汽车蓝皮书估价。

Key words and phrases

evolution	进化,演变
patent	专利;专利权;专利证书
enact	通过(法案等)
millennium	一千年
budget	预算
lease	租用,出租
test-drive	试验驾驶,试驾

peruse	细读, 研读
retail	零售
criterion	(*pl.* criteria) 标准, 准则, 原则
glossy	光滑的, 光彩夺目的, 有光泽的
sans	无, 没有
blemish	瑕疵, 斑点
diesel-fueled internal combustion engine	柴油内燃机
rule the roost	当头头, 充当首领, 主宰
back-up service	售后服务
smog test	烟雾测试

Exercises

1. Answer the following questions in English.

(1) Who was credited with building the world's first practical automobile to be powered by an internal combustion engine in 1885?

(2) Who improved the assembly line for automobile manufacturing?

(3) Did Rudolf Diesel invent the diesel-fueled internal combustion engine?

(4) Why did Japanese Government enact the Automobile Manufacturing Act in the 1930s?

(5) What do you need to follow before buying a new automobile?

2. Translate the following expressions into English.

(1) 四冲程发动机

(2) 充当首领,主宰
(3) 国际贸易差额
(4) 汽车蓝皮书
(5) 通用标准
(6) 运转状况

3. Translate the following sentences into English.

(1) 1885年,卡尔·奔驰制造出世界上第一辆以内燃机为动力的实用汽车。
(2) 20世纪初,美国的汽车公司处于主宰地位。
(3) 50年内,日本汽车技术取得了非凡的发展。
(4) 新千年汽车工业的未来依靠高科技电子、新型动力和人工智能的应用。
(5) 你应该在车辆特点、价格等方面做出一个彻底、全面的比较。
(6) 买车时售后服务也是应当考虑的。

■ **Passage D**

Car Logo

1. Buick:"tri-shield" (See Fig. 9-2)

Buick's famous "tri-shield" emblem, basically three shields inside a circle, can be traced directly to the ancestral coat of arms of the automakers' Scottish founder—David Dunbar Buick.

The description was interpreted as a red shield with a checkered silver and azure (light purplish blue) diagonal line running from the upper left corner to lower right, an antlered deer head with a jagged neckline in the upper right corner of the shield and a gold cross in the lower left corner. The cross had a hole in the center with the red of the shield showing through.

Fig. 9-2 Emblem of Buick

By 1959, the logo had undergone a major revision. In place of one shield, a tir-shield appeared, representing the three Buick models then being built: LeSabre, Invicta and Electra (all introduced as 1959 models).[2] Again, all of the original crest symbols and colors were retained, with the major difference being that instead of one shield, there were now the three overlapping shields in red, white (later silver gray) and blue.

2. **Benz-Mercedes**: "three-pointed star" (See Fig. 9-3)

Back in November 1890, Daimler-Motoren-Gesellschaft (DMG) was formed. In 1897, Jellinek made a journey to visit the Daimler factory and ordered his first Daimler car—a 6 hp belt-driven vehicle with two-cylinder engine, with a top speed of 24 km/h, which was finally delivered in October of the same year. As from 1899, Jellinek took the initiative to use the Daimler cars in order to participate in racing meetings—where he raced under his pseudonym, "Mercedes", the name of his daughter aged ten at the time.

|1899|1909|1916|
|1926|1996|

Fig 9-3 Emblem of Benz

At the beginning of April 1900, Jellinek made an agreement with DMG to develop a new engine "bearing the name Daimler-Mercedes", thereby introducing Jellinek's pseudonym as a product designation. Spanish origin, Mercedes mean "grace".

"Mercedes" was as a trade name legally registered on September 26. Although DMG now had a successful trade name, they still lacked a characteristic trademark. The company founder's two sons, Paul and Adolf Daimler, in charge of the business—remembered that their father, Gottlieb Daimler, had once marked a star, saying that this star would one day shine over his own factory symbolizing prosperity. The DMG board immediately accepted the proposal and in June 1909, the three-pointed was registered as trademarks. From 1910 onwards it began to appear at the front of the cars as a design feature on the radiator. The three-pointed star was supposed to symbolize Daimler's ambition of universal motorization—"on land, on water and in the air".

3. VOLVO: "I roll"

Assar Gabrielsson and Gustaf Larson were the two men behind Volvo. Gabrielsson began his career at SKF in Gothenburg. In time, he became the head of SKF's subsidiary in France and discovered that it was possible to sell Swedish ball-bearings at a lower price than the US suppliers could. It seems likely that it was here in France that Gabrielsson began to wonder whether Sweden might not be a suitable place to produce cars. Gustaf Larson was an engineer and designer. He had worked as a trainee in Coventry in England, where he was involved in the design of Morris engines. He then worked as an engineer at SKF in Gothenburg for three years. So, Assar Gabrielsson and Gustaf Larson had several opportunities to meet through their mutual employer. Perhaps it was at this time that the two of them started to develop the idea of Swedish car manufacture.

In July of 1926 the first chassis drawings were complete. They therefore decided to produce a test series of ten vehicles, nine open and one covered. The first test vehicles were produced in nine months and this time Gabrielsson succeeded in obtaining the financial support. SKF became interested. SKF also provided the factory premises and the name, Volvo. Volvo is Latin and means "I roll". So the preliminary work and the development period was over and 1927, when the first series-manufactured cars made their appearance, is officially recognised as the year in which Volvo started operations.[3]

4. VW : "people's car"

The "people's car" ("Volkswagen" in German) was the idea of car manufacturer Ferdinand Porsche, whose name was also associated with the superior car marque Porsche. He signed an agreement with German motor industry association in 1934 to produce a proper small, reliable car that ordinary people could afford, as opposed to the luxury motor cars which German companies preferred. Porsche had obviously looked over the sea at what Henry Ford had been able to achieve with the all-round, popular Model T Ford. The first model in its final form was completed in 1938. In 1961, production reached a million VW cars a year.

5. Ferrari: "prancing horse" (See Fig. 9-4)

All racing fans are very familiar with the famous Ferrari "prancing horse"symbol. The famous symbol of Ferrari is a black prancing horse on yellow background, usually with the letters S and F for Scuderia Ferrari. The horse was originally the symbol of Count Francesco Baracca, a legendary "asso" (ace) of the Italian air force during World War I, who painted it on the side of his planes.[5]

On June 17, 1923, Enzo Ferrari won a race and met Countess Paolina, mother of Baracca. The Count asked that he used the horse on his cars, suggesting that it would grant him good luck.

The prancing horse is now a trademark of Ferrari. After the great pilot died, Ferrari left the horse black in honour of him, upsides with Italian Flag, he added a yellow background because it was the symbolic color of his birthplace, Modena.

Fig 9-4 Emblem of Ferrari

Notes

[1] Buick's famous "tri-shield" emblem, basically three shields inside a circle, can be traced directly to the ancestral coat of arms of the automakers' Scottish founder—David Dunbar Buick.

别克著名的"三盾"标志是以一个圆圈中包含3个盾为基本的图案，它的由来可以直接追溯到汽车制造业的奠基人——苏格兰人大卫·邓巴·别克的家徽。

[2] In place of one shield, a tri-shield appeared, representing the three Buick models then being built: LeSabre, Invicta and Electra (all introduced as 1959 models).

由三盾替代了原来的一个盾标志，这3个盾分别代表别克的3种车型,它们是马刀(LeSabre)、英维克特(Invicta)、厄勒克特拉(Electra)(全是1959年的车型)。

[3] Volvo is Latin and means "I roll". So the preliminary work and the development period was over and 1927, when the first series-manufactured cars made their appearance, is officially recognised as the year in which Volvo started operations.

  Volvo 是拉丁语,意为"滚滚向前"。最初的工作和发展时期告一段落后,1927年,第一批汽车初次亮相,那一年被公认为 Volvo 开始运作的一年。

[4] The horse was originally the symbol of Count Francesco Baracca, a legendary "asso" (ace) of the Italian air force during World War I, who painted it on the side of his planes.

  这骏马原是弗朗西斯科·巴拉加伯爵的徽章,他是一位第一次世界大战中有传奇色彩的意大利空军王牌驾驶员,他的飞机侧翼画着腾马标志。

Key words and phrases

shield	盾(牌);盾形纹徽
ancestral	祖先的
azure	蔚蓝色的
antler	鹿角
jagged	凹凸不平的,有尖突的;锯齿状的
logo	标志,标识
crest	饰章,纹章
pseudonym	假名,化名
radiator	散热器
legendary	非常著名的,享有盛名的
ace	擅长……的人,精于……的人
coat of arms	盾形纹章,盾徽
three-pointed star	三叉星徽

Exercises

1. Answer the following questions in English.

(1) What's the logo of Buick?
(2) Why was the car named as "Mercedes"?
(3) What's the meaning of Volvo?
(4) What was the idea of car manufacturer Ferdinand Porsche?
(5) What does the logo of Ferrari come from?

2. Translate the following expressions into English.

(1) 盾形纹徽
(2) 皮带传动
(3) 三叉星徽
(4) 滚滚向前
(5) "大众的汽车"
(6) 腾马标志

3. Translate the following sentences into English.

(1) 三叉星徽表达了戴姆勒在陆、海、空3个领域实现机动化的夙愿。
(2) 汽车底盘的设计最终完成。因此,他们决定生产一个试用汽车系列,10辆汽车中9辆为敞开式,1辆为封闭式。
(3) 保时捷(波尔舍)把目光投向了海外,他要借鉴亨利·福特用功能齐全、时尚流行的T款式福特车赢得市场的经验。
(4) 法拉利的车标正是一匹黑色骏马,底色则是明亮的黄色,通常带有两个字母"S"和"F",它们是Scuderia Ferrari的首字母。
(5) "梅赛德斯"作为产品名称正式注册。

Application writing

商务信函
Business letters

商务信函包括信件、电子邮件、传真等，内容包括订单、询价、报价等。

较为正式的传真有固定的格式，格式中应包括发件人、收件人、单位名称、传真号、日期、页数、主题等，发件人在传真上签字也被视为国际惯例。

电子邮件不要求特别正式，但为了便于联系，通常应在邮件的最后提供联系方式，如发件人的姓名、职务、所在单位、电话号码、电子邮件地址、传真号码等。如：

（1）讨价还价

Dear Sir,

We have received your price lists and have studied it carefully. However, the price level in your quotation is too high for this market. If you are prepared to grant us a discount of 10% for a quantity of 200, we would agree to your offer. We hope to hear from you soon.

Yours truly,
John Chen

（2）正式提出订单

Dear Sir,

We have discussed your offer of 5% and accept it on the terms quoted. We are prepared to give your product a trial, provided you can guarantee delivery on or before the 20th of September. The enclosed order is given strictly on this condition. We reserve the right of refusal of delivery and/or cancellation of the order after this date.

Yours faithfully,
R. Smith

(3) 确认订单

Dear Sir,

Thank you very much for your order of June 15 for 200 Deer Mountain Bikes. We will make every possible effort to speed up delivery. We will advise you of the date of dispatch. We are at your service at all times.

                Yours faithfully,
                R. Smith

(4) 催款

Dear Mr. Bellon,

We are writing concerning the October account for $645 which was due and should have been cleared last month.

As you usually clear your account promptly, we wondered why the account was not paid. If you are experiencing any difficulties, please let me know as we may be able to help you. We look forward to hearing from you soon.

Attached please find a copy of the account.

                Yours sincerely,
                T. Lane

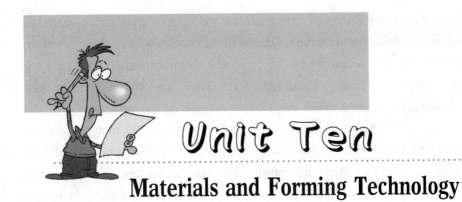

Unit Ten
Materials and Forming Technology

Goals

After studying the unit, you should be able to
- describe the types of materials and common metals.
- describe the structure and characteristics of stamping and punching dies.
- describe the application of plastics.
- distinguish thermoplastics and thermosets.
- understand the concept of mold CAD.

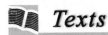 Texts

Passage A

Engineering Materials

1. Types of materials

Materials may be grouped in several ways. Scientists often classify materials by their state: solid, liquid or gas. They also separate them into organic and inorganic materials.

For industrial purposes, materials are divided into engineering materials and nonengineering materials. Engineering materials are those used in manufacture and become parts of products. Nonengineering materials are the chemicals, fuels, lubricants and other materials used in the manufacturing process which do not become part of the product.

This grouping is not exact. Engineering materials may be further subdivided into: metals, polymers, ceramics. A fourth type of material sometimes listed is called a composite. Materials in this type are made up of two or more materials from the engineering groups. Each of the materials in a composite retains its original characteristics. Examples of composites include wood, concrete, glass reinforced polyester and graphite polymer advanced composites.

2. Common metals

Pure metals are seldom used in common industrial products. Pure copper is used in electrical applications, automotive radiators and gaskets. Pure aluminum has applications in the chemical and electrical industries. However, most metals are alloys (combinations of two or more elements). There are over 2,500 different iron-carbon alloys (steels) and over 200 standard copper alloys including a number of brasses, bronzes and nickel silvers. Each of these alloys is identified by a code number.

Steel is an alloy of iron and carbon with other elements added to produce specific properties.

There are two general kinds of steels: carbon steel and alloy steel. Carbon steel contains only iron and carbon, while alloy steel contains some other "alloying elements" such as nickel, chromium, manganese, molybdenum, tungsten, vanadium, etc.

- Carbon steels

(1) Low carbon steel containing from 0.05% to 0.15% carbon; this steel is also known as machine steel.

(2) **Medium** carbon steel containing from 0.15% to 0.60% carbon.

(3) **High** carbon steel containing from 0.6% to 1.50% carbon; this

steel is sometimes called "tool steel".
- Alloy steels
(1) Special alloy steel, such as nickel, chromium steel;
(2) High-speed steel also known as self-hardening steel[1].

Carbon steels are the most common steels used in industry. The properties of these steels depend only on the percentage of carbon they contain. Low carbon steels are very soft and can be used for **bolts** and for machine parts that do not need strength.

Medium carbon steels are a better grade and stronger than low carbon steels. They are also more difficult to cut than low carbon steels.

High carbon steels may be **hardened** by heating it to a certain temperature and then quickly cooling in water. The more carbon the steel contains and the quicker the cooling is, the harder it becomes.[2] Because of its high strength and hardness, this grade of steel may be used for tools and working parts of machines.

But for some special uses, for example, for **gears**, **bearings**, springs, **shafts** and wire, carbon steels cannot be always used because they have no properties needed for these parts.

Some special alloy steels should be used for such parts because the alloying elements make them tougher, stronger, or harder than carbon steels. Some alloying elements cause steel to resist **corrosion**, and such steels are called **stainless steels**.[3] Stainless steels contain a high percentage of chromium. Chromium also makes steel harder. Nickel is used in steel to increase strength and toughness. Some alloying elements (such as chromium and tungsten) make the **grain** of steel finer, thus increasing the hardness and strength of steel, because the finer the grain is, the stronger the steel becomes.

Heat-resistant steel is made by adding some tungsten and molybdenum, while manganese increases the wear resistance of steel. Vanadium steels resist corrosion and can stand shocks and vibration.

Tools made of high-speed steels containing tungsten, chromium, vanadium, and carbon, may do the work at much higher speeds than carbon tool steels.[4]

Notes

[1] high-speed steel also known as self-hardening steel

高速钢，也称为自硬钢。

also known as self-hardening steel 为过去分词短语作定语，修饰 high-speed steel。

高速钢是一种含有钨、铬、钒等合金元素的高合金工具钢，它可以在空气中自行淬硬，因而称为 self-hardening steel，也称为风钢。

[2] The more carbon the steel contains and the quicker the cooling is, the harder it becomes.

钢的含碳量越高，冷却速度越快，钢就变得越硬。

"the + 比较级……（从句）+ the + 比较级……（主句）"结构表示"越……越……"之意。本句中的比较状语从句为"The more carbon the steel contains and the quicker the cooling is"，主句为"the harder it becomes"。句中第一个 the 和第三个 the 均为副词，分别引出两个并列的比较状语从句。在这种情况下，第一个 the 相当于 by so much，第三个 the 相当于 by that much。

[3] ... because the alloying elements make them tougher, stronger or harder than carbon steels. Some alloying elements cause steel to resist corrosion, and such steels are called stainless steels.

……因为合金元素比碳钢能提高钢的韧性、强度和硬度。有些合金元素能提高钢的耐蚀性，这种钢称作不锈钢。

句中的 make 和 cause 均为及物动词，它们的宾语分别为 them 和 steel。作为宾语 them 的补足语是形容词比较级 tougher, stronger, harder，作为宾语 steel 的补足语是不定式短语 to resist corrosion。stainless steels 是主语 such steels 的补足语。

[4] Tools made of high-speed steels containing tungsten, chromium, vanadium and carbon, may do the work at much higher speeds than

carbon tool steels.

用含有钨、铬、钒、碳的高速钢制成的刀具能以比碳素工具钢高得多的速度进行切削加工。

made of high-speed steel 是过去分词短语，修饰 tools，containing tungsten, chromium, vanadium and carbon 是现在分词短语作后置短语，修饰 high-speed steels。

Key words and phrases

nickel	镍
chromium	铬
manganese	锰
molybdenum	钼
tungsten	钨
vanadium	钒
medium	中等的,中号的
high-speed	高速的
bolt	螺栓
harden	(使)变硬,硬化
gear	齿轮;传动装置
heat-resistant	抗热的,耐热的
bearing	轴承
shaft	(机器的)轴
corrosion	腐蚀
stainless steel	不锈钢
grain	颗粒,细粒
tool steel	工具钢
self-hardening steel	自硬钢
heat-resistant steel	耐热钢

Exercises

1. Learn to speak.

Mr. Yang: Morning!
Mr. Smith: Morning!
Mr. Yang: Do you know about the kinds of steels?
Mr. Smith: Yes. There are two general kinds of steels: carbon steels and alloy steels.
Mr. Yang: Could you describe them in detail?
Mr. Smith: OK. Carbon steels contain only iron and carbon, while alloy steels contain some other "alloying elements" such as nickel, chromium, etc.
Mr. Yang: What can the carbon steels be used for?
Mr. Smith: The carbon steels contain low-, medium- and high-carbon steels, and can be used for bolts, tools and working parts of machines.
Mr. Yang: Then, what can the alloy steels be used for?
Mr. Smith: Alloy steels can be used for gears, bearings, springs and wires, etc., because the alloying elements make them tougher, stronger, or harder than carbon steels.
Mr. Yang: How about the tools which are made of high-speed steels?
Mr. Smith: The tools made of high-speed steels of alloy steels containing tungsten, chromium, vanadium and carbon, may do the work at much higher speeds than carbon tool steels.

2. Discuss the following questions in English.

(1) What methods are available for improving the hardness of high

carbon steels?

(2) What are the machine parts that do not need strength made of?

(3) How do the alloying elements such as chromium and tungsten increase the hardness and strength of steels?

3. Translate the following into English or Chinese.

(1) 碳钢和合金钢

(2) 材料的性能

(3) 高速钢

(4) heat-resistant steel

(5) self-hardening steel

(6) nickel steel

4. Write "T" (true) or "F" (false).

(1) Alloys having more than 0.6% carbon are called high-carbon steels. (　　)

(2) Alloys containing 0.15% (or less) carbon are called low-carbon steels. (　　)

(3) High-speed steels are sometimes called self-hardening steels. (　　)

(4) The properties of carbon steels depend not only on the percentage of carbon they contain, but also on the alloying elements. (　　)

(5) Steels contain more carbon than cast irons. (　　)

(6) Low-carbon steels are harder than high-carbon steels. (　　)

(7) Tools made of high-speed steels do the work at much lower speeds than carbon steels. (　　)

(8) Stainless steels contain some alloying elements which cause steels to resist corrosion. (　　)

Passage B

Stamping and Punching Dies, Compound Die Design

A compound die performs only cutting operations (usually **blanking** and **piercing**) which are completed during a single press **stroke**. A characteristic of compound dies is the inverted position of the blanking die and blanking **punch** which also functions as the piercing die. As shown in Fig. 10-1, the die is fastened to the **upper shoe** and the blanking punch having a **tapered hole** in the **lower shoe** for slug disposal.

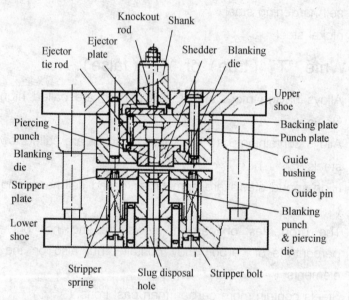

Fig. 10-1 A blanking and piercing compound die

The **guide pins** or posts are mounted in the lower shoe. The upper shoe contains bushing which slides on the guide pins. The assembly of the lower and upper shoes with guide pins and bushing is a **die set**. Die sets in many sizes and designs are commercially available.

On the upstroke of the press slide, the **knockout rod** of the press **strikes** the ejector plate, forcing the ejector tie rod and **shedder** downward, thus pushing the finished **workpiece** out of the blanking die.[1] Four special shoulder screws (**stripper bolts** commercially available) guide the stripper in its travel and retain it against the preload of its **springs**. The blanking die as well as the punch pad is screwed and doweled to the upper shoe.

1. Bending dies

Bending is the uniform straining of material (usually flat sheet or strip metal) around a straight axis which lies in the **neutral** plane and normal to the **lengthwise** direction of the sheet or strip. Metal flow takes place within the plastic range of the metal, so that the bend retains a **permanent set** after removal of the applied stress.[2] The **inner surface** of a bend is in compression; the **outer surface** is in **tension**. A pure bending action does not reproduce the exact shape of the punch and die in the metal; such a reproduction is one of forming. The neutral axis is the plane area in bend metal where all strain is zero.

2. Bending methods

Metal sheet or strip, supported by a V block, is forced by a **wedge-shaped** punch into the block. This method, termed V bending (Fig. 10-2), produces a bend having an included angle which may be **acute**, **obtuse**, or of 90°. Friction between a spring-loaded knurled pin in the vee of a die and

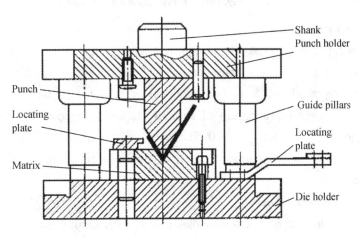

Fig. 10-2   V-bending die

the part will prevent or reduce side creep of the part during its bending.[3] Other methods are Z-bending (Fig. 10-3), edge bending and U-bending, etc.

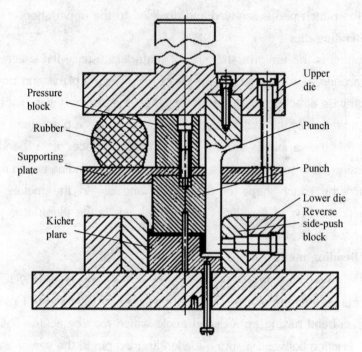

Fig. 10-3　Z-bending die

3. Drawing dies

Drawing is a process of changing a flat, precut metal blank into a hollow vessel without excessive **wrinkling**, thinning, or **fracturing**. The various forms produced may be **cylindrical** or **box-shaped** with straight or tapered sides or a combination of straight, tapered, or curved sides. The size of the parts may vary from 0.25 mm diameter or smaller to **aircraft** or automotive parts large enough to require the use of mechanical handing equipment.

4. Single-action Dies

The simplest type of drawing dies is one with only a punch and dies. One type of drawing die for use in a single-action press is shown in Fig. 10-4.

This die is plain single-action type where the punch pushes the metal blank into the die, using a spring-loaded pressure pad to control the metal flow. The punch has an **air vent** to eliminate suction which would hold the cup on the punch and damage the cup when it is stripped from the punch by the pressure pad. The sketch shows the pressure pad fitting the stop pin, which acts as a spacer that an even and proper pressure is exerted on the blank at all times. If the spring pressure pad is used without the stop pin, the more the springs are depressed, the greater the pressure exerted on the blank, thereby limiting the depth of draw.[4] Because of limited pressures obtainable, this type of die should be used with light-gage stock and shallow depths.

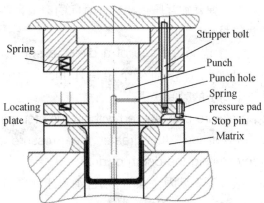

Fig. 10-4　First drawing die with elastic blank holder

Notes

[1] On the upstroke of the press slide, the knockout rod of the press strikes the ejector plate, forcing the ejector tie rod and shedder downward, thus pushing the finished workpiece out of the blanking die.

　　在冲压机滑块的向上行程中,冲压机的打料杆接触到推板,作用在连接推杆上的力使卸料装置下移,将冲压件从落料凹模中推出。

句中的 forcing the ejector tie rod and shedder downward 和 pushing the finished workpiece out of the blanking die 都是分词短语作状语，表示连续的动作。

[2] Metal flow takes place within the plastic range of the metal, so that the bend retains a permanent set after removal of the applied stress.

因为(弯曲时)金属流动发生在金属塑性变形范围内，所以，去除施加的外力后，弯曲将保持永久的变形。

句中 so that 引导的是结果状语从句，applied 是 stress 的定语。

[3] Friction between a spring-loaded knurled pin in the vee of a die and the part will prevent or reduce side creep of the part during its bending.

V形模具内的弹簧加载压销和零件之间的摩擦力，将阻止或减少弯曲时零件边缘的移动。

句中的介词短语 in the vee of a die 作 a spring-loaded knurled pin 的定语，between 连接的两个短语作 friction 的定语，during its bending 是整个句子的时间状语。

[4] If the spring pressure pad is used without the stop pin, the more the springs are depressed, the greater the pressure exerted on the blank, thereby limiting the depth of draw.

如果弹压板没有安装限位螺钉，那么弹簧压缩得越多，板料承受的压力就越大，这将限制拉深的程度。

句中 If 引导的是条件状语从句，the more ... the greater ... 表示"越……越……"，thereby limiting the depth of draw 作状语，表示结果。

Key words and phrases

die	模具，冲模，压模
blanking	落料，下料
piercing	冲孔
stroke	(打、击等的)一下，一击；冲程

strike	撞,撞击,碰撞
punch	冲床,打孔机,穿孔器
tapered	(使)逐渐变窄的;锥形的,尖削的,渐缩的
shedder	脱模装置
workpiece	工件
spring	弹簧
neutral	中立的;中性的
lengthwise	纵长的,纵向长的
tension	拉伸,张力
wedge-shaped	楔形的,V形的
acute	锐角的
obtuse	钝角的
friction	摩擦;摩擦力
knurled	滚花的,压花的;有节的,有凸边的
wrinkle	皱纹,皱褶
fracture	破裂,断裂,打断
cylindrical	圆柱形的,圆筒状的
box-shaped	盒形的
aircraft	飞机,航空器
eliminate	排除,消除
stamping and punching die	冲压模
compound die	复合模
upper shoe	上模座
lower shoe	下模座
guide pin	导料销
die set	模架
knockout rod	打料杆

stripper bolt	卸料螺钉
bending die	弯曲模
permanent set	永久应变(变形)
inner surface	内表面
outer surface	外表面
knurled pin	压销
drawing die	拉深模,深冲模
air vent	通气孔

Exercises

1. Translate the following into Chinese.

Metal sheet or strip supported by a V-shape block is forced by a wedge-shaped punch into the block. This method termed V-shape bending produces a bend having an included angle, which may be acute, obtuse, or of 90°. Friction between a spring-loaded knurled pin in the vee will prevent or reduce side creep of the part during its bending. Other methods are Z-bending, edge bending and U-bending, etc.

Extended reading

Passage C

Classification and Application of Plastics

Plastics are generally divided into the two categories of **thermoplastic(s)** and **thermosets** (or thermostet plastics) plastic.

1. Thermoplastics

We noted earlier that, in the **amorphous** structure of a **polymer**, the bonds between adjacent long-chain molecule (secondary bonds) are much weaker than the **covalent** bonds (primary bonds) within each molecule.[1] Hence, it is the strength of the secondary bonds that determines the overall strength of the polymer. Linear and branched polymers have weak secondary bonds.

If we raise the temperature of this polymer above the glass-transition temperature, we'll find that it becomes softer and easier to form or to mold into a shape.[2] The **mobility** of the long molecules (**thermal vibrations**) increases at Tg and above. If this polymer is now cooled, it returns to its original hardness and strength. In other words, the process is **reversible**.

Polymers that exhibit this behaviors are known as thermoplastics. Typical examples are **acrylics**, **nylon**, **ployethlene**, and polyvinyl **chloride**.

2. Thermosets

When the long-chain molecules in a polymer are cross-linked in a three-dimensional (**spatia**) network, the structure becomes in effect one giant molecule with strong covalent bonds.[3] Cross-linking is done by the **polymerization** processes. Because of the nature of the bonds, the strength and hardness of such a polymer is not affected by temperature.

These polymers are known as thermosets because, during polymerization under heat and pressure, the network is completed and the shape of the part is **permanently** set (curing). Unlike in thermoplastics, this reaction is irreversible and the polymer cannot be recycled.[4] However, if the temperature is increased sufficiently, the thermosetting polymer begins to **decompose**, char, and degrade. Thermosetting polymers do not have a sharply defined glass-transition temperature. Commonly, thermosetting **resins** become rubbery and compliant across a narrow temperature range.

The response of a thermosetting plastic to temperature can be compared to boiling an egg or **baking** a cake.[5] Once the cake is baked and cooled, reheating it will not change its shape, and if the temperature is too high, it will burn. On the other hand, the response of a thermoplastic can also be compared to ice cream. It can be softened, refrozen, and resoftened a number of times. It can be molded into shapes, frozen, and then softened again to be remolded into a different shape.

A typical example of a thermosetting plastic is **phenolic**, which is a product of the reaction between phenol and **formaldehyde**.[6] Typical products of this polymer are the handles on cooking pots and pans and electrical components such as switches.

The polymerization process for thermosets generally takes place in two stages. The first one is at the chemical plant, where the molecules are partially polymerized into linear chains. The second stage is at the part-producting plant, where the cross-linking is completed under heat and pressure during the molding of the part.

Thermosetting plastics generally posses better mechanical, thermal, chemical, and electrical resistance and better dimensional **stability** than thermoplastics.

Notes

[1] We noted earlier that, in the amorphous structure of a polymer, the bonds between adjacent long-chain molecule (secondary bonds) are much weaker than the covalent bonds (primary bonds) within each molecule.

我们在前面已经提到过,在聚合物非晶态结构中,相邻的长链分子之间的键的结合力要弱于长链内部分子之间的共价键(主键)。

句中 that 是从属连词,引导宾语从句,作动词 note 的宾语。much weaker 中的 much 放在形容词比较级之前,表程度,译为"……得多"。

[2] If we raise the temperature of this polymer above the glass-transition temperature, we'll find that it becomes softer and easier to form or to mold into a shape.

如果把这种聚合体的温度提升至玻璃(态)化温度之上,我们就会发现聚合体变得更软且更易成型或模塑成型。

此句为含有 if 引导的条件状语从句的复合句,主句中包含一个由 that 引导的宾语从句,作 find 的宾语。

[3] When the long-chain molecules in a polymer are cross-linked in a three-dimensional (spatial) network, the structure becomes in effect one giant molecule with strong covalent bonds.

聚合体中长链分子以三维(空间)网络交联时,其结构变成一个带有强大共价联结物的巨型分子。

句中 in effect 的意思是"实际上,事实上"。cross-link 意为"交联"。

[4] These polymers are known as thermosets because, during polymerization under heat and pressure, the network is completed and the shape of the part is permanently set (curing). Unlike in thermoplastics, this reaction is irreversible and the polymer cannot be recycled.

这种聚合物被称为热固材料,因为在加热和加压下进行的聚合过程中,网状结构被形成,产品的形状被永久地固定下来。这种反应是不可逆的,并且这种聚合物也不能被回收,这与热塑性塑料不一样。

be known as 的意思是"被认为是"。句中 unlike, irreversible 中"un-"、"ir-"均为否定前缀,表示"不",如 unable(不能的,不会的);unacceptable(无法接受的,不受欢迎的), irreal(不真实的,虚构的), irregular(不规则的,无规律的)。

[5] The response of a thermosetting plastic to temperature can be compared to boiling an egg or baking a cake.

热固性材料对温度的反应可比作煮鸡蛋或烤面包。

句中短语 be compared to 中的 to 为介词,后接名词或动名词形式。类似的短语如 look forward to,意为"期待,期望,期盼"。

[6] A typical example of a thermosetting plastic is phenolic, which is a product of the reaction between phenol and formaldehyde.

热固性塑料的典型实例是酚醛塑料,这是(苯)酚和甲醛反应的产物。

句中 which 是关系代词,引导非限定性定语从句。

Key words and phrases

thermoplastic(s)	热塑(性)塑料
thermoster	热固(性)材料
amorphous	无定形的,〈化〉非晶态的,非晶形的
polymer	聚合物,多聚体
covalent	共价的
mobility	流动能力;移动的能力
Tg(glass-transition temperature)	玻璃(态)化温度
reversible	可逆的
acrylics	丙烯酸类材料
nylon	尼龙
polyethlene	〈化〉聚乙烯
chloride	聚氯乙烯
spatial	空间的
polymerization	聚合
permanently	永久地,持久地
reaction	反应,回应;化学反应
decompose	(使)分解
char	烧焦,(使)烧黑
degrade	(使)退化,降解,分解;降低……身份
resin	树脂;合成树脂
bake	(在烤炉里)烘烤,焙;(将某物)烤硬
phenolic	〈化〉酚的,苯酚的
formaldehyde	〈化〉甲醛

stability 稳定(性),稳固(性)
thermal vibration 热振动

Exercises

1. Answer the following questions according to the passage above.

(1) What are thermoplastics?
(2) What are theromosets?

2. Fill in the blanks with proper words.

(1) If we now raise the temperature of the polymer above the glass-transition temperature, we'll find _____ it becomes softer and easier to form or to mold into a shape.
(2) _____ the nature of the bonds, the strength and hardness of such a polymer is not affected by temperature.
(3) However, _____ the temperature is increased sufficiently, the thermosetting polymer begins to decompose, char, and degrade.
(4) Once the cake is baked and cooled, reheating it will not change its shape, and if the temperature is too _____, it will burn.
(5) A typical example of a thermosetting plastic is phenolic, _____ is a product of the reaction between phenol and formaldehyde.

Passage D

The Computer in Die Design

The term CAD is alternately used to mean computer-aided design and computer-aided drafting. Actually it can mean either one or both of those concepts, and the tool designer will have occasion to use it in both forms.

CAD computer-aided design means using the computer and **peripheral devices** to simplify and enhance the design process. CAD **computer-aided drafting** means using the computer and peripheral devices to produce the **documentation** and **graphics** for the design process.[1] This documentation usually includes such things as **preliminary drawing**, **working drawing**, parts lists, and **design calculations**.

A CAD system, whether taken to mean computer-aided design system or computer-aided drafting system, consists of three basic components: hardware, software, and users. The hardware components of a typical CAD system include a **processor**, a system display, a **keyboard**, a **digitizer**, and a **plotter**. The software components of a CAD system consist of the programs which allow it to perform design and drafting functions. The user is the tool designer who uses the hardware and software to simplify and enhance the design process.

The broad-based emergence of CAD on an **industry-wide** basis did not begin to **materialize** until the 1980s. However, CAD as a concept is not new. Although it has changed over the years, CAD had its beginnings during the middle 1950s. Some of the first computers included **graphics displays**. Now a graphics display is a part of every CAD system.

Graphics displays represented the first real step toward combining the world of tool design and the computer together. With the **advent** of the **digitizing tablet** in the early 1960s, CAD hardware as we know it today began to **take shape**. The development of computer graphics software followed soon after these hardware developments.

Early CAD systems were large, heavy, and expensive. They were so expensive in fact that only the largest companies could afford them. During the late 1960s, CAD was looked on as an interesting, but **impractical novelty** that had only limited potential in tool design applications. However, with the introduction of the **silicon chip** during the 1970s, computers began to take their place in the world of tool design.

Integrated circuits on silicon chips allowed full-scale computers to be packaged in small **consoles** no larger than television sets.[2] These minicomputers had all of the characteristics of all full-scale computers, but they were smaller and considerably less expensive. Even smaller computers called microcomputers followed soon after.

The 1970s saw continued advances in CAD hardware and software technology. So much so that by the beginning of the 1980s, making and marketing CAD systems had become a growth industry. Also, CAD has been transformed from its status of impractical novelty to its new status as one of the most important inventions to date.[3] By 1980, numerous CAD systems were available ranging in sizes from microcomputer systems to large minicomputer and mainframe systems.

As soon as the customer has transferred the part design to the moldmaker via the appropriate interface, the mold designer can design the mold around the part. The designer determines the size of the mold, whether moving parts are required, and the layout of cooling lines and gate locations, etc., all in relation to the part geometry. All aspects of the mold design are stored in the computer and can be retrieved at any time.

Notes

[1] CAD computer-aided drafting means using the computer and peripheral devices to produce the documentation and graphics for the design process.

CAD 计算机辅助绘图是指用计算机和外围设备(外部设备)来产生

设计过程的文件和图样。

本句为简单句,主语是 CAD computer-aided drafting,谓语是 means,宾语是 using the computer and peripheral devices to produce the documentation and graphics for the design process。

[2] Integrated circuits on silicon chips allowed full-scale computers to be packaged in small consoles no larger than television sets.

硅片上的集成电路使得在控制台上被组装起来的大规模集成计算机不比电视机大。

allowed ... to do ... 意为"允许……做……" no larger than ... 意为"不比……大,与……大小一样"。

[3] Also, CAD has been transformed from its status of impractical novelty to its new status as one of the most important inventions to date.

另外,CAD 已经从过去的华而不实变成如今最重要的发明之一。

be transformed from ... to ... 意为"由…… 转变成……"

Key words and phrases

peripheral	外围的,周边的;与计算机相连的
documentation	(计算机等辅助的)文献编制, 文件(编集)
graphics	图样,图案,绘图
processor	处理器,处理机
keyboard	键盘
digitizer	数字转换器
plotter	(计算机)绘图仪,描绘器
broad	板,电路板
industry-wide	工业领域
materialize	实现,发生;突然显现
advent	出现,到来
impractical	不明智的,不现实的

novelty	新颖(性);事物;新奇(感)新奇
console	(机器、电子设备等的)控制台,操纵台,仪表板
computer-aided drafting	计算机辅助绘图
preliminary drawing	预制图
working drawing	工作图
design calculation	设计计算
graphics display	图形显示
digitizing tablet	数字化板
take shape	成形
silicon chip	硅片
integrated circuit	集成电路

Exercises

1. Answer the following questions according to the passage above.

(1) What are the two different interpretations of the term CAD? What are the differences between these two concepts?

(2) What are the three basic components included in a typical CAD system?

(3) What are the hardware components included in a typical CAD system?

(4) What function does CAD have when the moldmaker designs mold?

2. Put the following words into English.

计算机辅助设计　　外围设备（外设）　　硬件　　　　软件
用户　　　　　　　工具设计领域　　　　集成电路　　微机
小型机　　　　　　巨型机　　　　　　　工业领域　　CAD 系统
预制图　　　　　　图形显示

Application writing

产品制造合同

Product manufacturing contract

产品制造合同是指企业与制造商签订合同，并由该制造商生产产品，而企业负责产品销售的一种合作形式。利用制造合同，企业将全部或部分生产的工作与责任转移给了合同的对方，以便将精力集中在营销上，因而是一种有效的扩展国际市场的方式。这种模式的优点还在于，实行制造合同的企业不仅可以输出技术或商标等无形资产，而且还可以输出劳务和管理等生产要素，以及部分资本。

1. 产品制造合同的格式

产品制造合同一般应该包括以下几个方面：
（1）产品名称、规格、数量、价格（一般还包括产品使用的材料）；
（2）质量要求、技术标准等；
（3）付款方式；
（4）交货时间；
（5）责任承担；
（6）双方协议签订日期、法人代表、单位名称。

2. 产品制造合同的示例

模具制造合同

Part A：(Purchaser)

Party B：(Mold Maker)

This contract is hereby made and entered into between the purchaser (hereinafter referred as Party A) and mold maker (hereinafter referred as Party B) on the basis of equality and mutual benefit and through friendly negotiations. Terms and conditions stipulate below:

1. Mold name, specification, steel for the cavities, and price listed as below:

Name	Specification	Steel for cavity & cores	Unit price	Total amount	Notes
		Total			

2. All the mold prices are FOB Guangzhou.

3. The lead time of mold making: The lead time will be ___days, from the date which is confirmed by Party B having received the 50% deposit to the delivery the first consignment.

4. Mold design & manufacturing requirements:

(1) Party B should design & make the molds to the samples or the drawings provided by Party A, and on form to Party A's requirements.

(2) The cooling water system should be appropriate so that the mold can be cooled enough.

(3) The mold design should be approved by Party A before the mold making starts.

(4) If necessary, Party A should prove the specification and date of the injection machine which will work with the mold.

(5) The part should fall down automatically when the mold runs normally except some special parts.

5. Payment terms: 50% of the total amount should be prepaid as deposit before the projects of the mold making starts, and the balance should paid after the mold have been checked and approved. Party B shall ship the said goods to Party A after confirming receipt of the total amount.

6. Responsibility:

(1) If Party B doesn't make the mold according to the samples or drawings provided by Party A, Party A has the right to ask Party B to repair

or rework the mold.

(2) Party B should accept to be forfeited money by Party A if Party B can't finish the mold in the appointed lead time. Then 0.1% of the total mold price will be cut down as forfeiture of per day's delay.

(3) If they need to change the mold or the part after the files used to build the mold and mold design are approved, Party A should pay for the additional changes, while Party B will be free of the responsibility if the lead time delays. And the price of changes and the update lead time should be negotiated by the both parties.

7. The contract shall be written in Chinese. And all the terms and interpretation should be subject to the Chinese version. This contract should be submitted by Chinese law. The other details that are not listed in this contract should be kindly negotiated by both parties.

Party A: Party B:
Address: Address:
Representative: Representative:
(Signature)_____   (Signature)_____
Date(yyyy-mm-dd)   Date(yyyy-mm-dd)